Monongalia County Cemetery,
Morgantown, West Virginia
1928-1955

Cynthia Harper

Harpers Global LLC

The Town Pauper's Burial
By: Charles G. Eastman

Bury him there-
No matter where!
Hustle him out of the way!
Trouble enough
We have with such stuff-
Taxes and money to pay!

Bury him there-
No matter where!
Off in some corner at best!
There's no need of stones,
Above his old bones
Nobody'll ask where they rest.

Bury him there-
No matter where!
None by his death are bereft;
Stopping to pray?
Shovel away!
We still have enough of them left.

Bury him there-
No matter where!
An y where out of the way
Trouble enough
We have with such stuff-
Taxes and money to pay.

## Acknowledgements

To my daughter, Kyleigh Blanchard, thank you for contributing your art work for this book. I love you with all of my heart. I am blessed to be your momma.

Thank you to my parents, Rev. Larry C. Harper and Edith Morton Harper, for your love and guidance in life.

Harpers Global LLC
Morgantown, WV
Cover design by Cindie Harper
Cover photograph by Cindie Harper
Artwork by Kyleigh Blanchard

ISBN-10: 173396570X
ISBN-13: 978-1733965705
ISBN 9781733965712 (ebook)

In Memorium


For those who are buried in the Monongalia County
Cemetery in unmarked graves.
May Their Souls Rest In Peace.

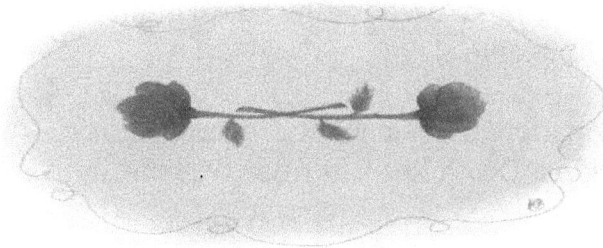

## Introduction

The Monongalia County Cemetery is located on West Run Road in Morgantown, Monongalia County, West Virginia. This cemetery was once known as Potter's Field or the local pauper cemetery. This cemetery is where they buried people who did not belong to a church or have a space in one of the private cemeteries. The county cemetery was often used for the burial of unknown or indigent people.

The information in this book was compiled using West Virginia Death Records from 1928 through 1955.

The cemetery is typically mowed. The parking area is sparse. The cemetery is difficult to see from the road.

The Monongalia Cemetery marker is difficult to read because the stone has been damaged. It appears to read as follows:.

Monongalia
County
Cemetery
Erected  --
By
The Monongalia
County Commission
Eugene --llaro
President
Joseph E Kun
Commissioner
James A Ashburn
Commissioner

There are 324 unmarked white marker stones that are laid out in rows.

There are seven marked graves as follows:

Herman Cannon
Ohio
PVT 330 N G BN
92D
November 19 1933 (or 1938)

Wilbert L Whitehair
West Virginia
CPL Ordnance Department
World War II
July 13 1906    July 24 1963

William Cobb
1903-1963

Mary Strosnider
1880-1950

Harry M Phillips
1940-1988

Juanita Rife
(funeral home marker)


Pearl Groves
Phillips
1898-1969

# 1928

Name: George Armit
Birth Date: Unknown
Birth Place: Bulgaria
Death Date: 27 Dec 1928
Burial Date: 29 Dec 1928
Race: W
Gender: M
Cemetery: Monongalia County, W.V. Cemetery


Name: Andrew Balluk
Birth Date: Unknown
Birth Place: Unknown
Death Date: 12 Nov 1928
Burial Date: 13 Nov 1928
Race: W
Gender: M
Cemetery: Monongalia County, W.V. Cemetery


Name: Tony Bessork
Birth Date: Unkown
Birth Place: Lithuania
Death Date: 23 Nov 1928
Burial Date: 27 Nov 1928
Race: W
Gender: M
Cemetery: Monongalia County, W.V. Cemetery

Name: Dollie Champ
Birth Date: Unknown
Birth Place: Harrisville, WV
Death Date: 07 Mar 1928
Burial Date: 08 Mar 1928
Race: W
Gender: F
Cemetery: Monongalia County, W.V. Cemetery


Name: Andy Cullen
Birth Date: Unknown
Birth Place: Unknown
Death Date: 17 Mar 1928
Burial Date: Unknown
Race: W
Gender: M
Cemetery: Monongalia County, W.V. Cemetery


Name: John Cushion
Birth Date: Unknown
Birth Place: Unknown
Death Date: 22 Dec 1928
Burial Date: 24 Dec 1928
Race: W
Gender: M
Cemetery: Monongalia County, W.V. Cemetery

Name: Ike Davis
Birth Date: Unknown
Birth Place: Unknown
Death Date: 23 Jun 1928
Burial Date: Unknown
Race: Colored
Gender: M
Cemetery: Monongalia County, W.V. Cemetery


Name: Vernon Howard Garner Edwards
Birth Date: 10 Jan 1928
Birth Place: Westover, WV
Death Date: 14 Mar 1928
Burial Date: 17 Mar 1928
Race: Colored
Gender: M
Cemetery: Monongalia County, W.V. Cemetery


Name: Mike Gautley
Birth Date: Unknown
Birth Place: Unknown
Death Date: 25 Apr 1928
Burial Date: 26 Apr 1928
Race: W
Gender: M
Cemetery: Monongalia County, W.V. Cemetery

Name: Tony Gotenguski
Birth Date: Unknown
Birth Place: Poland
Death Date: 01 Jul 1928
Burial Date: 02 Jul 1928
Race: W
Gender: M
Cemetery: Monongalia County, W.V. Cemetery


Name: American Helmic
Birth Date:
Birth Place:
Death Date: 18 Feb 1928
Burial Date: 21 Feb 1928
Race: W
Gender: F
Cemetery: Monongalia County, W.V. Cemetery


Name: Harvey Jackson
Birth Date: 04 Jan 1928
Birth Place: Scotts Run
Death Date: 07 Oct 1928
Burial Date: 099 Oct 1928
Race: Colored
Gender: M
Cemetery: Monongalia County, W.V. Cemetery

Name: Steve Kerinsky
Birth Date: Unknown
Birth Place: Romania Europe
Death Date: 15 Jun 1928
Burial Date: 16 Jun 1928
Race: W
Gender: M
Cemetery: Monongalia County, W.V. Cemetery


Name: Infant Mahlee
Birth Date: 10 Jan 1928
Birth Place: Unknown
Death Date: 11 Jan 1928
Burial Date: 12 Jan 1928
Race: W
Gender: M
Cemetery: Monongalia County, W.V. Cemetery


Name: Millad M. Menear
Birth Date: 03 Mar 1927
Birth Place: WV
Death Date: 28 Dec 1928
Burial Date: 31 Dec 1928
Race: W
Gender: M
Cemetery: Monongalia County, W.V. Cemetery

Name: Alfred Mills
Birth Date: Unknown
Birth Place: Unknown
Death Date: 16 Jul 1928
Burial Date: 19 Jul 1928
Race: W
Gender: M
Cemetery: Monongalia County, W.V. Cemetery


Name: Vasile Onai
Birth Date: Unknown
Birth Place: Romania
Death Date: 26 Jan 1928
Burial Date: 28 Jan 1928
Race: W
Gender: M
Cemetery: Monongalia County, W.V. Cemetery


Name: Mike Paulich
Birth Date: Unknown
Birth Place: Unknown
Death Date: 13 Mar 1928
Burial Date: 17 Mar 1928
Race: W
Gender: M
Cemetery: Monongalia County, W.V. Cemetery

Name: John Rusko
Birth Date: Unknown
Birth Place: Lithuania
Death Date: 15 Jan 1928
Burial Date: 17 Jan 1928
Race: W
Gender: M
Cemetery: Monongalia County, W.V. Cemetery


Name: Henry Smith
Birth Date: Unknown
Birth Place: Waynesburgh, Va
Death Date: 07 Nov 1928
Burial Date: 08 Nov 1928
Race: Colored
Gender: M
Cemetery: Monongalia County, W.V. Cemetery


Name: Joe Smith
Birth Date: Unknown
Birth Place: Unknown
Death Date: 22 Oct 1928
Burial Date: 23 Oct 1928
Race: W
Gender: M
Cemetery: Monongalia County, W.V. Cemetery

Name: Mary Valovich
Birth Date: 23 March 1928
Birth Place: Maidsville, WV
Death Date: 04 Oct 1928
Burial Date: 06 Oct 1928
Race: W
Gender: F
Cemetery: Monongalia County, W.V. Cemetery


Name: James Walker
Birth Date: 12 Feb 1882
Birth Place: Alabama
Death Date: 05 Sep 1928
Burial Date: 09 Sep 1928
Race: Black
Gender: M
Cemetery: Monongalia County, W.V. Cemetery


Name: Ruben Walker
Birth Date: 04 July 1888
Birth Place: Oklahoma
Death Date: 18 Jan 1928
Burial Date: 20 Jan 1928
Race: Colored
Gender: M
Cemetery: Monongalia County, W.V. Cemetery

Name: Mamie Whitlock
Birth Date: Unknown
Birth Place: Unknown
Death Date: 03 Apr 1928
Burial Date: 05 Apr 1928
Race: Colored
Gender: F
Cemetery: Monongalia County, W.V. Cemetery


Name: Katherine Willes
Birth Date: 12 April 1928
Birth Place: Clarksburg, WV
Death Date: 27 Sep 1928
Burial Date: 29 Sept 1928
Race: W
Gender: F
Cemetery: Monongalia County, W.V. Cemetery


Name: Caldonia Williams
Birth Date: Unknown
Birth Place: Unknown
Death Date: 17 May 1928
Burial Date: 23 May 1928
Race: Colored
Gender:  F
Cemetery: Monongalia County, W.V. Cemetery

Name: Gussie Williams
Birth Date: Unknown
Birth Place: Kentucky
Death Date: 30 Nov 1928
Burial Date: 03 Dec 1928
Race: Colored
Gender: F
Cemetery: Monongalia County, W.V. Cemetery


Name: Sam Wilson
Birth Date: 04 Jul 1871
Birth Place: South Carolina
Death Date: 12 Jun 1928
Burial Date: 14 Jun 1928
Race: Colored
Gender: M
Cemetery: Monongalia County, W.V. Cemetery

# 1929

Name: Steve Bialko
Birth Date: Unknown
Birth Place: Russia
Death Date: 19 November 1929
Burial Date: 21 November 1929
Race: W
Gender: M
Cemetery: Monongalia County, W.V. Cemetery


Name: Jack Boyd
Birth Date: Unknown
Birth Place: Va.
Death Date: 14 September 1929
Burial Date: 15 September 1929
Race: Black
Gender: M
Cemetery: Monongalia County, W.V. Cemetery


Name: Mrs. Estella Brice
Birth Date: 1886
Birth Place: Ala.
Death Date: 24 July 1929
Burial Date: 26 July 1929
Race: C
Gender: F
Cemetery: Monongalia County, W.V. Cemetery

Name: Maggie Call
Birth Date: 09 July 1891
Birth Place: W.Va.
Death Date: 27 February 1929
Burial Date: 04 March 1929
Race: W
Gender: F
Cemetery: Monongalia County, W.V. Cemetery


Name: Joseph Cwbiak
Birth Date: Unknown
Birth Place: Poland
Death Date: 08 September 1929
Burial Date: 12 September 1929
Race: W
Gender:  M
Cemetery: Monongalia County, W.V. Cemetery


Name: Romney U. Davis
Birth Date: 24 December 1891
Birth Place: East India
Death Date: 20 June 1929
Burial Date: 25 June 1929
Race: C
Gender: M
Cemetery: Monongalia County, W.V. Cemetery

Name: Will George
Birth Date: Unknown
Birth Place: Unknown
Death Date: 26 August, 1929
Burial Date: 27 August 1929
Race: C
Gender: M
Cemetery: Monongalia County, W.V. Cemetery


Name: Mathew Grohar
Birth Date: Unknown
Birth Place: Czechoslavakia
Death Date: 13 August 1929
Burial Date: 15 August 1929
Race: W
Gender:  M
Cemetery: Monongalia County, W.V. Cemetery


Name: Florence Hill
Birth Date: Unknown
Birth Place: Unknown
Death Date: 12 January 1929
Burial Date: 16 January 1929
Race: C
Gender: F
Cemetery: Monongalia County, W.V. Cemetery

Name: George Holland
Birth Date: Unknown
Birth Place: Ala.
Death Date: 06 September 1929
Burial Date: 07 September 1929
Race: C
Gender:  M
Cemetery: Monongalia County, W.V. Cemetery


Name: Myrtle Lee Johnson
Birth Date: 22 June 1918
Birth Place: Pa.
Death Date: 29 January 1929
Burial Date: 31 January 1929
Race: C
Gender: F
Cemetery: Monongalia County, W.V. Cemetery


Name: Samuel Johnson
Birth Date: Unknown
Birth Place: W.Va.
Death Date: 21 March 1929
Burial Date: 24 March 1929
Race: W
Gender: M
Cemetery: Monongalia County, W.V. Cemetery

Name: Malcome Kepps
Birth Date: 29 April 1929
Birth Place: Monesson
Death Date: 26 August 1929
Burial Date: 27 August 1929
Race: W
Gender: M
Cemetery: Monongalia County, W.V. Cemetery


Name: Mary Jane Lemley
Birth Date: Unknown
Birth Place: W.Va.
Death Date: 11 February 1929
Burial Date: 13 February 1929
Race: W
Gender:  F
Cemetery: Monongalia County, W.V. Cemetery


Name: Herlbert H. Menear
Birth Date: Unknown
Birth Place: W.Va.
Death Date: 18 July 1929
Burial Date: 20 July 1929
Race: W
Gender:M
Cemetery: Monongalia County, W.V. Cemetery

Name: Mike Morosky
Birth Date: Unknown
Birth Place: Unknown
Death Date: 11 June 1929
Burial Date: 14 June 1929
Race: W
Gender:M
Cemetery: Monongalia County, W.V. Cemetery


Name: Jammie Morrise
Birth Date: 08 March 199
Birth Place: Ga.
Death Date: 05 January 1929
Burial Date: 15 January 1929
Race: C
Gender: M
Cemetery: Monongalia County, W.V. Cemetery


Name: Columbine May Nair
Birth Date: 09 April 1928
Birth Place: W.Va.
Death Date: 19 January 1929
Burial Date: 21 January 1929
Race: W
Gender: F
Cemetery: Monongalia County, W.V. Cemetery

Name: Eli Otis
Birth Date: Unknown
Birth Place:  Austria
Death Date: 16 October 1929
Burial Date: 18 October 1929
Race: W
Gender: M
Cemetery: Monongalia County, W.V. Cemetery


Name: James Posten
Birth Date: Unknown
Birth Place: Va.
Death Date: 11 August 1929
Burial Date: 12 August 1929
Race: C
Gender: M
Cemetery: Monongalia County, W.V. Cemetery


Name: Wallace Winfield Riley
Birth Date: 1927
Birth Place: Bretz, Preston County, W.Va.
Death Date: 06 August 1929
Burial Date: 08 August 1929
Race: W
Gender: M
Cemetery: Monongalia County, W.V. Cemetery

Name: Oliver Robert
Birth Date: Unknown
Birth Place: Unknown
Death Date: 07 January 1929
Burial Date: 08 January 1929
Race: W
Gender: M
Cemetery: Monongalia County, W.V. Cemetery


Name: James Rush
Birth Date: 19 March 1918
Birth Place: Virginia
Death Date: 17 July 1929
Burial Date: 19 July 1929
Race: C
Gender: M
Cemetery: Monongalia County, W.V. Cemetery


Name: Charles Stephenson
Birth Date: Unknown
Birth Place: Unknown
Death Date: 03 January 1929
Burial Date: 12 January 1929
Race: C
Gender: M
Cemetery: Monongalia County, W.V. Cemetery

Name: Wm Valentine
Birth Date: Unknown
Birth Place: Unknown
Death Date: 25 January 1929
Burial Date: 27 January 1929
Race: W
Gender: M
Cemetery: Monongalia County, W.V. Cemetery


Name: Joe Unknown
Birth Date: Unknown
Birth Place: Unknown
Death Date: 03 March 1929
Burial Date: 04 March 1929
Race: W
Gender: M
Cemetery: Monongalia County, W.V. Cemetery


Name: Steve Vargo
Birth Date: Unknown
Birth Place: Lithuania Europe
Death Date: 12 November 1929
Burial Date: 15 November 1929
Race: W
Gender: M
Cemetery: Monongalia County, W.V. Cemetery

Name: Joe Venkuss
Birth Date: Unknown
Birth Place: Lithuania
Death Date: 12 November 1929
Burial Date: 13 November 1929
Race: W
Gender: M
Cemetery: Monongalia County, W.V. Cemetery


Name: Ida May Winemiller
Birth Date: 21 July 1929
Birth Place: W.Va.
Death Date: 23 July 1929
Burial Date: 24 July 1929
Race: W
Gender: F
Cemetery: Monongalia County, W.V. Cemetery


Name: Delma Ray Wright
Birth Date: 23 April 1927
Birth Place: W.Va.
Death Date: 15 January 1929
Burial Date: 16 January 1929
Race: W
Gender: M
Cemetery: Monongalia County, W.V. Cemetery

Name: William Yanulavich
Birth Date: Unknown
Birth Place: Russia
Death Date: 27 March 1929
Burial Date: 28 March 1929
Race: W
Gender:M
Cemetery: Monongalia County, W.V. Cemetery

# 1930

Name: Joe Allison
Birth Date: 18 July 1875
Birth Place: England
Death Date: 16 February 1930
Burial Date: 19 February 1930
Race: White
Gender: Male
Cemetery: Monongalia County, W.V. Cemetery


Name: Charles Bateman
Birth Date: Unknown
Birth Place: Unknown
Death Date: 25 February 1930
Burial Date: 18 March 1930
Race: White
Gender: Male
Cemetery: Monongalia County, W.V. Cemetery

Name: John Berry
Birth Date: Unknown
Birth Place: Unknown (Alabama?)
Death Date: 23 September 1930
Burial Date: 26 September 1930
Race: "Colord"
Gender: Male
Cemetery: Monongalia County, W.V. Cemetery


Name: Fedeman Betencourt
Birth Date: 08 March 1930
Birth Place: Monongalia County, W.Va.
Death Date: 19 September 1930
Burial Date: 20 September 1930
Race: Mexican
Gender: Male
Cemetery: Monongalia County, W.V. Cemetery


Name: Bertha Anna Biekel
Birth Date: 20 January 1930
Birth Place: West Virginia
Death Date: 31 July 1930
Burial Date: 01 August 1930
Race: White
Gender: Female
Cemetery: Monongalia County, W.V. Cemetery

Name: Ellis Croston
Birth Date: 22 March 1880
Birth Place: West Virginia
Death Date: 02 May 1930
Burial Date: 03 May 1930
Race: White
Gender: Male
Cemetery: Monongalia County, W.V. Cemetery


Name: Phillip J. Davy
Birth Date: 13 May 1930
Birth Place: West Virginia
Death Date: 22 May 1930
Burial Date: 24 May 1930
Race: White
Gender: Male
Cemetery: Monongalia County, W.V. Cemetery


Name: Robert Floyd Douglas
Birth Date: 17 May 1930
Birth Place: Osage, W.Va
Death Date: 22 July 1930
Burial Date: 23 July 1930
Race: "Colored"
Gender: Male
Cemetery: Monongalia County, W.V. Cemetery

Name: Frank Fernanda
Birth Date: Unknown
Birth Place: Spain
Death Date: 17 May 1930
Burial Date: 19 May 1930
Race: White
Gender: Male
Cemetery: Monongalia County, W.V. Cemetery


Name: Rose Georgia Foster
Birth Date: 29 June 1930
Birth Place: Morgantown, W.Va.
Death Date: 17 December 1930
Burial Date: 19 December 1930
Race: White
Gender: Female
Cemetery: Monongalia County, W.V. Cemetery


Name: John Hudy
Birth Date: 1881
Birth Place: Poland
Death Date: 01 May 1930
Burial Date: 11 May 1930
Race: White
Gender: Male
Cemetery: Monongalia County, W.V. Cemetery

Name: Zanie Lewis
Birth Date: Unknown
Birth Place: Unknown
Death Date: 30 August 1930
Burial Date: 01 September 1930
Race: "Colored"
Gender: Female
Cemetery: Monongalia County, W.V. Cemetery


Name: Infant McCargish
Birth Date: 06 September 1930
Birth Place: West Virginia
Death Date: 07 September 1930
Burial Date: 08 September 1930
Race: White
Gender: Male
Cemetery: Monongalia County, W.V. Cemetery


Name: Mike Mitrekovich
Birth Date: Unknown
Birth Place: Austria
Death Date: 21 December 1930
Burial Date: 22 December 1930
Race: White
Gender: Male
Cemetery: Monongalia County, W.V. Cemetery

Name: August Molenski
Birth Date: 1869
Birth Place: "Russian Poland"
Death Date: 28 December 1930
Burial Date: 29 December 1930
Race: White
Gender: Male
Cemetery: Monongalia County, W.V. Cemetery


Name: Mildred Lowise Pardee
Birth Date: 12 May 1929
Birth Place: W.Va.
Death Date: 03 October 1930
Burial Date: 05 October 1930
Race: White
Gender: Female
Cemetery: Monongalia County, W.V. Cemetery


Name: Mike Raspi
Birth Date: 19 October 1930
Birth Place: West Virginia
Death Date: 11 November 1930
Burial Date: 12 November 1930
Race: White
Gender: Male
Cemetery: Monongalia County, W.V. Cemetery

Name: Edward Russick
Birth Date: Unknown
Birth Place: Slavia
Death Date: 28 October 1930
Burial Date: 31 October 1930
Race: White
Gender: Male
Cemetery: Monongalia County, W.V. Cemetery


Name: Joe Salsey
Birth Date: Unknown
Birth Place: Unknown
Death Date: 17 March 1930
Burial Date: 19 March 1930
Race: White
Gender: Male
Cemetery: Monongalia County, W.V. Cemetery


Name: Ernest Severe
Birth Date: July 1878
Birth Place: Maryland
Death Date: 05 October 1930
Burial Date: 08 October 1930
Race: White
Gender: Male
Cemetery: Monongalia County, W.V. Cemetery

Name: William Simms
Birth Date: Unknown
Birth Place: Clarksburg, W.Va.
Death Date: 13 July 1930
Burial Date: 15 July 1930
Race: White
Gender: Male
Cemetery: Monongalia County, W.V. Cemetery

Name: Hermon Howard Miller Slider
Birth Date: 05 March 1930
Birth Place: Morgantown, W.Va.
Death Date: 09 March 1930
Burial Date: 12 March 1930
Race: White
Gender: Male
Cemetery: Monongalia County, W.V. Cemetery


Name: Mike Stadnect
Birth Date: Unknown
Birth Place: Russia
Death Date: 28 October 1930
Burial Date: 31 October 1930
Race: Russian
Gender: Male
Cemetery: Monongalia County, W.V. Cemetery

Name: John Stetson
Birth Date: Unknown
Birth Place: Unknown
Death Date: 22 March 1930
Burial Date: 23 March 1930
Race: "Black"
Gender: Male
Cemetery: Monongalia County, W.V. Cemetery


Name: Leatrice Joy Strozier
Birth Date: 01 August 1930
Birth Place: Pursglove, W.Va
Death Date: 06 August 1930
Burial Date: 06 August 1930
Race: "Colored"
Gender:  Female
Cemetery: Monongalia County, W.V. Cemetery


Name: Frank Tallis
Birth Date: Unknown
Birth Place: Austria
Death Date: 27 December 1930
Burial Date: 30 December 1930
Race: White
Gender: Male
Cemetery: Monongalia County, W.V. Cemetery

Name: Sam Truchane
Birth Date: Unknown
Birth Place: Unknown
Death Date: 25 January 1930
Burial Date: 27 January 1930
Race: White
Gender: Male
Cemetery: Monongalia County, W.V. Cemetery


Name: Unknown
Birth Date: Unknown
Birth Place: Unknown
Death Date: Body Found 17 April 1930
Burial Date: 18 April 1930
Race: White
Gender: Male
Cemetery: Monongalia County, W.V. Cemetery

Name: Tom Vucsovic
Birth Date: Unknown
Birth Place: "Probably Italy"
Death Date: 15 March 1930
Burial Date: 18 March 1930
Race: White
Gender: Male
Cemetery: Monongalia County, W.V. Cemetery

Name: Betty Jean Wilson
Birth Date: 31 March 1930
Birth Place: West Virginia
Death Date: 28 July 1930
Burial Date: 29 July 1930
Race: White
Gender: Female
Cemetery: Monongalia County, W.V. Cemetery


Name: Ruhl Whytsell
Birth Date: 07 July 1906
Birth Place: Braxton County, W.Va.
Death Date: 22 February 1930
Burial Date: 24 February 1930
Race: White
Gender: Male
Cemetery: Monongalia County, W.V. Cemetery

# 1931

Name: Lewis Allen
Birth Date: Unknown
Birth Place: Georgia
Death Date: 28 July 1931
Burial Date: 29 July 1931
Race: "Colored"
Gender: Male
Cemetery: Monongalia County, W.V. Cemetery


Name: Clara Dale Anastio
Birth Date: 14 July 1930
Birth Place: Virginia
Death Date: 07 August 1931
Burial Date: 08 August 1931
Race: W
Gender: F
Cemetery: Monongalia County, W.V. Cemetery


Name: Deloris Chinovsky
Birth Date: 02 May 1931
Birth Place: Monongalia County, W.Va.
Death Date: 02 October 1931
Burial Date: 03 October 1931
Race: W
Gender: F
Cemetery: Monongalia County, W.V. Cemetery

Name: Henry Cobbs
Birth Date: 23 April 1885
Birth Place: W.Va.
Death Date: 03 June 1931
Burial Date: 05 June 1931
Race: White
Gender: Male
Cemetery: Monongalia County, W.V. Cemetery


Name: Lonnie Jr. Dubose
Birth Date: 04 May 1904
Birth Place: Alabama
Death Date: 04 June 1931
Burial Date: 06 June 1931
Race: C
Gender: M
Cemetery: Monongalia County, W.V. Cemetery


Name: Walter Feagen
Birth Date: Unknown
Birth Place: Unknown
Death Date: 20 July 1931
Burial Date: 21 July 1931
Race: "Colored"
Gender: Male
Cemetery: Monongalia County, W.V. Cemetery

Name: Lucille Flowers
Birth Date: 1913
Birth Place: Alabama
Death Date: 12 July 1931
Burial Date: 15 July 1931
Race: "Colored"
Gender: Female
Cemetery: Monongalia County, W.V. Cemetery


Name: William Hawkins
Birth Date: Unknown
Birth Place: Unknown
Death Date: 29 July 1931
Burial Date: 31 July 1931
Race: "Colored"
Gender: Male
Cemetery: Monongalia County, W.V. Cemetery


Name: Mike Kaluga
Birth Date: Unknown
Birth Place: Russia
Death Date: 02 May 1931
Burial Date: 07 May 1931
Race: White
Gender: Male
Cemetery: Monongalia County, W.V. Cemetery

Name: Elizabeth Parker
Birth Date: 10 February 1881
Birth Place: W.Va.
Death Date: 29 May 1931
Burial Date: 31 May 1931
Race: White
Gender: Female
Cemetery: Monongalia County, W.V. Cemetery


Name: Dorothy Dale Simmons
Birth Date: 08 May 1931
Birth Place: Monongalia County, W.Va.
Death Date: 12 June 1931
Burial Date: 13 June 1931
Race: White
Gender: Female
Cemetery: Monongalia County, W.V. Cemetery


Name: Tom Smith
Birth Date: Unknown
Birth Place: Unknown
Death Date: 03 July 1931
Burial Date: 06 July 1931
Race: "Colored"
Gender: Male
Cemetery: Monongalia County, W.V. Cemetery

Name: Carl Stakow
Birth Date: Unknown
Birth Place: Russia
Death Date: about 30 May 1931
Burial Date: 21 June 1931
Race: Russian
Gender: Male
Cemetery: Monongalia County, W.V. Cemetery


Name: Dowe Watson
Birth Date: 1855
Birth Place: W.Va.
Death Date: 21 May 1931
Burial Date: 23 May 1931
Race: White
Gender: Male
Cemetery: Monongalia County, W.V. Cemetery

# 1932

Name: Andy Becken
Birth Date: Unknown
Birth Place: Lithuania
Death Date: 12 May 1932
Burial Date: 19 May 1932
Race: W
Gender: M
Cemetery: Monongalia County, W.V. Cemetery


Name: Myrtle Blocker
Birth Date: Unknown
Birth Place: Pa
Death Date: 08 January 1932
Burial Date: 11 January 1932
Race: B
Gender: F
Cemetery: Monongalia County, W.V. Cemetery


Name: Alex Dardo
Birth Date: Unknown
Birth Place: Unknown
Death Date: 26 June 1932
Burial Date: 29 June 1932
Race: W
Gender: M
Cemetery: Monongalia County, W.V. Cemetery

Name: George Dargus
Birth Date: Unknown
Birth Place: Lithuania
Death Date: 11 June 1932
Burial Date: 13 June 1932
Race: W
Gender: M
Cemetery: Monongalia County, W.V. Cemetery


Name: Joe Deme
Birth Date: Unknown
Birth Place: Austria
Death Date: 27 September 1932
Burial Date: 28 September 1932
Race: W
Gender: M
Cemetery: Monongalia County, W.V. Cemetery


Name: Frank Dulkay
Birth Date: Unknown
Birth Place: Unknown
Death Date: 13 March 1932
Burial Date: 14 March 1932
Race: W
Gender: M
Cemetery: Monongalia County, W.V. Cemetery

Name: Daniel Fain
Birth Date: 01 May 1893
Birth Place: Cartersville
Death Date: 03 April 1932
Burial Date: 06 April 1932
Race: C
Gender: M
Cemetery: Monongalia County, W.V. Cemetery


Name: Nick Filis
Birth Date: Unknown
Birth Place: Greece
Death Date: 15 June 1932
Burial Date: 16 June 1932
Race: W
Gender: M
Cemetery: Monongalia County, W.V. Cemetery


Name: Perry Ghoston
Birth Date: Unknown
Birth Place: Alabama
Death Date: 12 November 1932
Burial Date: 15 November 1932
Race: C
Gender: M
Cemetery: Monongalia County, W.V. Cemetery

Name: Joe Growvish
Birth Date: Unknown
Birth Place: Austria
Death Date: 30 September 1932
Burial Date: 01 October 1932
Race: W
Gender: M
Cemetery: Monongalia County, W.V. Cemetery


Name: Walter Hill
Birth Date: Unknown
Birth Place: Alabama
Death Date: 13 May 1932
Burial Date: 15 May 1932
Race: C
Gender: M
Cemetery: Monongalia County, W.V. Cemetery


Name: Mike Izenbeluk
Birth Date: Unknown
Birth Place: Unknown
Death Date: 02 July 1932
Burial Date: 07 July 1932
Race: W
Gender: M
Cemetery: Monongalia County, W.V. Cemetery

Name: Infant Katchan
Birth Date: 09 August 1932
Birth Place: Brewer Hill, W.Va.
Death Date: 09 August 1932
Burial Date: 09 August 1932
Race: W
Gender: F
Cemetery: Monongalia County, W.V. Cemetery


Name: Frank Koral
Birth Date: Unknown
Birth Place: Russia
Death Date: 18 April 1932
Burial Date: 21 April 1932
Race: W
Gender: M
Cemetery: Monongalia County, W.V. Cemetery


Name: Andy Kovatch
Birth Date: Unknown
Birth Place: Hungary
Death Date: 19 July 1932
Burial Date: 22 July 1932
Race: W
Gender: M
Cemetery: Monongalia County, W.V. Cemetery

Name: Mary Rosie Marsh
Birth Date: 05 February 1932
Birth Place: Monongalia County, W.Va.
Death Date: 01 November 1932
Burial Date: 02 November 1932
Race: W
Gender: F
Cemetery: Monongalia County, W.V. Cemetery


Name: Radi Margaret Mayliew
Birth Date: 05 November 1932
Birth Place: Arnettsville, W.Va
Death Date: 17 November 1932
Burial Date: 18 November 1932
Race: W
Gender: F
Cemetery: Monongalia County, W.V. Cemetery


Name: John Paulish
Birth Date: Unknown
Birth Place: Unknown
Death Date: 20 June 1932
Burial Date: 21 June 1932
Race: W
Gender: M
Cemetery: Monongalia County, W.V. Cemetery

Name: J. L Perkins
Birth Date: Unknown
Birth Place: Alabama
Death Date: 01 June 1932
Burial Date: 03 June 1932
Race: "Colored"
Gender: M
Cemetery: Monongalia County, W.V. Cemetery


Name: Barto Petick
Birth Date: Unknown
Birth Place: Unknown
Death Date: 04 June 1932
Burial Date: 05 June 1932
Race: W
Gender: M
Cemetery: Monongalia County, W.V. Cemetery


Name: Nancie Carroll Reese
Birth Date: 26 May 1932
Birth Place: Osage, W.Va.
Death Date: 27 May 1932
Burial Date: 28 May 1932
Race: W
Gender: F
Cemetery: Monongalia County, W.V. Cemetery

Name: Willis Franklin Riley
Birth Date: 13 February 1932
Birth Place: Morgantown, W.Va.
Death Date: 25 May 1932
Burial Date: 26 May 1932
Race: W
Gender: M
Cemetery: Monongalia County, W.V. Cemetery


Name: Wilma Frances Riley
Birth Date: 13 February 1932
Birth Place: Morgantown, W.Va.
Death Date: 29 June 1932
Burial Date: 30 June 1932
Race: W
Gender: F
Cemetery: Monongalia County, W.V. Cemetery


Name: Alice Lowise Shock
Birth Date: 24 May 1932
Birth Place: Morgantown, W.Va.
Death Date: 24 May 1932
Burial Date: 25 May 1932
Race: W
Gender: F
Cemetery: Monongalia County, W.V. Cemetery

Name: George Scarlotis
Birth Date: Unknown
Birth Place: Greece
Death Date: 03 October 1932
Burial Date: 06 October 1932
Race: W
Gender: M
Cemetery: Monongalia County, W.V. Cemetery


Name: Debby Stockwell
Birth Date: 15 August 1867
Birth Place: Braxton County, W.Va.
Death Date: 26 December 1932
Burial Date: 28 December 1932
Race: W
Gender: F
Cemetery: Monongalia County, W.V. Cemetery


Name: Bendi Uska
Birth Date: Unknown
Birth Place: Unknown
Death Date: 11 May 1932
Burial Date: 13 May 1932
Race: W
Gender: M
Cemetery: Monongalia County, W.V. Cemetery

Name: John Voras
Birth Date: Unknown
Birth Place: Unknown
Death Date: 24 February 1932
Burial Date: 25 February 1932
Race: W
Gender: M
Cemetery: Monongalia County, W.V. Cemetery


Name: Frances Wilson
Birth Date: 16 April 1912
Birth Place: South Carolina
Death Date: 01 January 1932
Burial Date: 03 January 1932
Race: C
Gender: F
Cemetery: Monongalia County, W.V. Cemetery


Name: Victor Cecil Winemiller
Birth Date: 21 July 1928
Birth Place: Hilderbrand, W.Va.
Death Date: 16 December 1932
Burial Date: 18 December 1932
Race: W
Gender: M
Cemetery: Monongalia County, W.V. Cemetery

Name: Pete Wiselones
Birth Date: Unknown
Birth Place: Lithuania
Death Date: 21 November 1932
Burial Date: 25 November 1932
Race: W
Gender: M
Cemetery: Monongalia County, W.V. Cemetery

Name: Antonia Jr Zbrosky
Birth Date: 27 December 1927
Birth Place: West Virginia
Death Date: 07 May 1932
Burial Date: 10 May 1932
Race: White
Gender: M
Cemetery: Monongalia County, W.V. Cemetery

# 1933

Name: Vera Lee Armstead
Birth Date: 04 June 1933
Birth Place: Monongalia County, W.V.
Death Date: 04 June 1933
Burial Date: 05 June 1933
Race: W
Gender: F
Cemetery: Monongalia County, W.V. Cemetery


Name: Alex Boko
Birth Date: Unknown
Birth Place: Poland
Death Date: 24 July 1933
Burial Date: 29 July 1933
Race: W
Gender: M
Cemetery: Monongalia County, W.V. Cemetery


Name: Charles Earl Bollinger
Birth Date: Unknown
Birth Place: Grafton, W.Va
Death Date: 28 November 1933
Burial Date: 01 December 1933
Race: W
Gender: M
Cemetery: Monongalia County, W.V. Cemetery

Name: Matilda Hawkins Brooks
Birth Date: 06 January 1865
Birth Place: Missouri
Death Date: 21 June 1933
Burial Date: 24 June 1933
Race: W
Gender: F
Cemetery: Monongalia County, W.V. Cemetery


Name: Herman Cannon
Birth Date: Unknown
Birth Place: Tennessee
Death Date: 19 November 1933
Burial Date: 22 November 1933
Race: C
Gender: M
Cemetery: Monongalia County, W.V. Cemetery


Name: John Fitzpatrick
Birth Date: Unknown
Birth Place: Unknown
Death Date: 26 February 1933
Burial Date: 27 February 1933
Race: W
Gender: M
Cemetery: Monongalia County, W.V. Cemetery

Name: Jack Flenes
Birth Date: Unknown
Birth Place: Lithuania
Death Date: 29 March 1933
Burial Date: 30 March 1933
Race: W
Gender: M
Cemetery: Monongalia County, W.V. Cemetery


Name: John Fredasky
Birth Date: Unknown
Birth Place: Austria
Death Date: 23 May 1933
Burial Date: 24 May 1933
Race: W
Gender: M
Cemetery: Monongalia County, W.V. Cemetery


Name: Pete Gaunaw
Birth Date: Unknown
Birth Place: Unknown
Death Date: 02 November 1933
Burial Date:  03 November 1933
Race: W
Gender: M
Cemetery: Monongalia County, W.V. Cemetery

Name: Frank Getter
Birth Date: 23 March 1884
Birth Place: Spottenbergh, S.C.
Death Date: 25 April 1933
Burial Date: 27 April 1933
Race: C
Gender: M
Cemetery: Monongalia County, W.V. Cemetery


Name: Raymond Hart
Birth Date: 01 June 1910
Birth Place: Cleveland, Ohio
Death Date: 07 June 1933
Burial Date: 09 June 1933
Race: C
Gender: M
Cemetery: Monongalia County, W.V. Cemetery

Name: James Otis Herndon
Birth Date: 09 February ----
Birth Place: W.Va.
Death Date: 10 December 1933
Burial Date: 12 December 1933
Race: W
Gender: M
Cemetery: Monongalia County, W.V. Cemetery

Name: Lewis Jones
Birth Date: Unknown
Birth Place: Unknown
Death Date: 20 February 1933
Burial Date: 22 February 1933
Race: C
Gender: M
Cemetery: Monongalia County, W.V. Cemetery


Name: Samuel Walker Knight
Birth Date: 19 July 1933
Birth Place: Booth, W.Va.
Death Date: 19 July 1933
Burial Date: 21 July 1933
Race: W
Gender: M
Cemetery: Monongalia County, W.V. Cemetery


Name: Paul Kovack
Birth Date: Unknown
Birth Place: "Probably Austria"
Death Date: 05 October 1933
Burial Date: 09 October 1933
Race: W
Gender: M
Cemetery: Monongalia County, W.V. Cemetery

Name: John Kravitski
Birth Date: Unknown
Birth Place: Russia
Death Date: 18 July 1933
Burial Date: 19 July 1933
Race: W
Gender: M
Cemetery: Monongalia County, W.V. Cemetery


Name: Robert Ramdan L. Lightcap
Birth Date: 09 April 1933
Birth Place: Bertha Hill, W.Va
Death Date: 08 October 1933
Burial Date: 10 October 1933
Race: W
Gender: M
Cemetery: Monongalia County, W.V. Cemetery


Name: Josh Love
Birth Date: 17 February 1876
Birth Place: Charleston, S.C.
Death Date: 13 October 1933
Burial Date: 15 October 1933
Race: C
Gender: M
Cemetery: Monongalia County, W.V. Cemetery

Name: Hazel Ruth Mace
Birth Date: 04 May 1931
Birth Place: Morgantown, W.Va.
Death Date: 11 February 1933
Burial Date: 12 February 1933
Race: W
Gender: F
Cemetery: Monongalia County, W.V. Cemetery


Name: John R. Matthews
Birth Date: Unknown
Birth Place: Barbour County, W.Va.
Death Date: 27 October 1933
Burial Date: 30 October 1933
Race: W
Gender: M
Cemetery: Monongalia County, W.V. Cemetery


Name: William Eugene Melady
Birth Date: 10 November 1932
Birth Place: West Virginia
Death Date: 02 January 1933
Burial Date: 04 January 1933
Race: W
Gender: M
Cemetery: Monongalia County, W.V. Cemetery

Name: Johne Ezera Alfred Menear
Birth Date: Unknown
Birth Place: Preston County, W. Va.
Death Date: 05 November 1933
Burial Date: 09 November 1933
Race: W
Gender: M
Cemetery: Monongalia County, W.V. Cemetery


Name: Charles Miller
Birth Date: Unknown
Birth Place: Unknown
Death Date: 07 April 1933
Burial Date: 08 April 1933
Race: W
Gender: M
Cemetery: Monongalia County, W.V. Cemetery


Name: Louis Nelrs
Birth Date: Unknown
Birth Place: Austria Hungaria
Death Date: 14 March 1933
Burial Date: 23 March 1933
Race: W
Gender: M
Cemetery: Monongalia County, W.V. Cemetery

Name: Charley Payne
Birth Date: Unknown
Birth Place: Unknown
Death Date: 20 October 1933
Burial Date: 25 October 1933
Race: C
Gender: M
Cemetery: Monongalia County, W.V. Cemetery


Name: Hannah Payntes
Birth Date: 07 June 1845
Birth Place: Unknown
Death Date: 17 August 1933
Burial Date: 20 August 1933
Race: W
Gender: F
Cemetery: Monongalia County, W.V. Cemetery


Name:  Martin Persuchia
Birth Date: Unknown
Birth Place: Russia
Death Date: 01 May 1933
Burial Date: 03 May 1933
Race: W
Gender: M
Cemetery: Monongalia County, W.V. Cemetery

Name: Mabel Riley
Birth Date: 28 August 1893
Birth Place: Louisville, Kentucky
Death Date: 16 May 1933
Burial Date: 18 May 1933
Race: W
Gender: F
Cemetery: Monongalia County, W.V. Cemetery


Name: Maude Irene Riley
Birth Date: 13 May 1933
Birth Place: Stone Mines, W.Va
Death Date: 18 September 1933
Burial Date: 20 September 1933
Race: W
Gender: F
Cemetery: Monongalia County, W.V. Cemetery


Name: Geelena Robinson
Birth Date: 15 August 1914
Birth Place: Alabama
Death Date: 05 December 1933
Burial Date: 08 December 1933
Race: C
Gender: F
Cemetery: Monongalia County, W.V. Cemetery

Name: Infant of Frank W. Rodgers
Birth Date: 13 June 1933
Birth Place: Morgantown, W.Va.
Death Date: 13 June 1933
Burial Date: 15 June 1933
Race: W
Gender: M
Cemetery: Monongalia County, W.V. Cemetery


Name: Steve Rubo
Birth Date: Unknown
Birth Place: Austria
Death Date: 03 June 1933
Burial Date: 06 June 1933
Race: W
Gender: M
Cemetery: Monongalia County, W.V. Cemetery


Name: George Serena
Birth Date: Unknown
Birth Place: Hungary
Death Date: 07 February 1933
Burial Date: 08 February 1933
Race: W
Gender: M
Cemetery: Monongalia County, W.V. Cemetery

Name: Roman Silasky
Birth Date: Unknown
Birth Place: Poland
Death Date: 31 December 1933
Burial Date: 03 January 1934
Race: W
Gender: M
Cemetery: Monongalia County, W.V. Cemetery


Name: Margie Smith
Birth Date: Unknown
Birth Place: Purlaska, Va.
Death Date: 28 September 1933
Burial Date: 03 October 1933
Race: C
Gender: F
Cemetery: Monongalia County, W.V. Cemetery


Name: Nick StarRovich
Birth Date: 1872
Birth Place: Austria
Death Date: 26 August 1933
Burial Date: 29 August 1933
Race: W
Gender: M
Cemetery: Monongalia County, W.V. Cemetery

Name: Annie Conner Taylor
Birth Date: Unknown
Birth Place: Booster, Alabama
Death Date: 30 September 1933
Burial Date: 04 October 1933
Race: C
Gender: F
Cemetery: Monongalia County, W.V. Cemetery


Name: Toney Trybus
Birth Date: Unknown
Birth Place: Poland
Death Date: 01 October 1933
Burial Date: 03 October 1933
Race: W
Gender: M
Cemetery: Monongalia County, W.V. Cemetery


Name: Frank Turkl
Birth Date: Unknown
Birth Place: Jugo- Slavakia
Death Date: 01 June 1933
Burial Date: 03 June 1933
Race: W
Gender: M
Cemetery: Monongalia County, W.V. Cemetery

Name: Margaret N. Uphold
Birth Date: 26 December 1933
Birth Place: Maidsville, W.V.
Death Date: 28 December 1933
Burial Date: 29 December 1933
Race: W
Gender: F
Cemetery: Monongalia County, W.V. Cemetery


Name: Unknown Unknown
Birth Date: Unknown
Birth Place: Unknown
Death Date: 18 June 1933
Burial Date: 18 June 1933
Race: W
Gender: M
Cemetery: Monongalia County, W.V. Cemetery

# 1934

Name: John Borotka
Birth Date: Unknown
Birth Place: Unknown
Death Date: 15 March 1934
Burial Date: 21 March 1934
Race: W
Gender: M
Cemetery: Monongalia County, W.V. Cemetery


Name: Rose J. Brown
Birth Date: 19 May 1934
Birth Place:
Death Date: 01 October 1934
Burial Date: 03 October 1934
Race: W
Gender: F
Cemetery: Monongalia County, W.V. Cemetery


Name: Dave Calhaun
Birth Date: 03 August
Birth Place: Alabama
Death Date: 20 August 1934
Burial Date: 23 August 1934
Race: W
Gender: M
Cemetery: Monongalia County, W.V. Cemetery

Name: Joe Carmish
Birth Date: Unknown
Birth Place: "Old Country"
Death Date: 08 December 1934
Burial Date: 14 December 1934
Race: W
Gender: M
Cemetery: Monongalia County, W.V. Cemetery


Name: John Casta
Birth Date: Unknown
Birth Place: Unknown
Death Date: 18 May 1934
Burial Date: 20 May 1934
Race: W
Gender: M
Cemetery: Monongalia County, W.V. Cemetery


Name: Chas. Cosma
Birth Date: Unknown
Birth Place: Possibly Hungary
Death Date: 09 June 1934
Burial Date: 10 June 1934
Race: W
Gender: M
Cemetery: Monongalia County, W.V. Cemetery

Name: Sam Philopovich Fille
Birth Date: Unknown
Birth Place: Austria
Death Date: 20 November 1934
Burial Date: 21 November 1934
Race: W
Gender: M
Cemetery: Monongalia County, W.V. Cemetery


Name: Ben Gabriel
Birth Date: Unknown
Birth Place: Alabama
Death Date: 03 July 1934
Burial Date: 07 July 1934
Race: C
Gender: M
Cemetery: Monongalia County, W.V. Cemetery


Name: Grace Glendening
Birth Date: 21 April 1913
Birth Place: W.Va.
Death Date: 07 March 1934
Burial Date: 10 March 1934
Race: W
Gender: F
Cemetery: Monongalia County, W.V. Cemetery

Name: Junior Tate
Birth Date: November
Birth Place: Rivesville, W.Va.
Death Date: 14 May 1934
Burial Date: 16 May 1934
Race: C
Gender: M
Cemetery: Monongalia County, W.V. Cemetery


Name: Steve Tate
Birth Date: Unknown
Birth Place: Austria
Death Date: 09 April 1934
Burial Date: 13 April 1934
Race: W
Gender: M
Cemetery: Monongalia County, W.V. Cemetery


Name: Eli Todoroff
Birth Date: 21 April
Birth Place: Bulgara
Death Date: 09 June 1934
Burial Date: 11 June 1934
Race: W
Gender: M
Cemetery: Monongalia County, W.V. Cemetery

Name: Reuben Jefferson
Birth Date: Unknown
Birth Place: Unknown
Death Date: 04 November 1934
Burial Date: 05 November 1934
Race: C
Gender: M
Cemetery: Monongalia County, W.V. Cemetery


Name: George Kamach
Birth Date: Unknown
Birth Place: Unknown
Death Date: 25 September 1934
Burial Date: 28 September 1934
Race: W
Gender: M
Cemetery: Monongalia County, W.V. Cemetery


Name: Pete Kowasa
Birth Date: Unknown
Birth Place: Unknown
Death Date: 17 July 1934
Burial Date: 21 July 1934
Race: W
Gender: M
Cemetery: Monongalia County, W.V. Cemetery

Name:Isarel Edward Lightcap
Birth Date: 18 October 1842
Birth Place: Bolliver, Pa.
Death Date: 17 January 1934
Burial Date: 20 January 1934
Race: W
Gender: M
Cemetery: Monongalia County, W.V. Cemetery


Name: Ray Leon Luzader
Birth Date: 04 April 1934
Birth Place: Chaplin; Colliers Hill, Osage, W.Va.
Death Date: 12 September 1934
Burial Date: 14 September 1934
Race: W
Gender: M
Cemetery: Monongalia County, W.V. Cemetery


Name: Walter Benton Mayhew
Birth Date: 04 September 1933
Birth Place: Monongalia County, W.Va.
Death Date: 02 January 1934
Burial Date: 03 January 1934
Race: W
Gender: M
Cemetery: Monongalia County, W.V. Cemetery

Name: Barbara Joan Miller
Birth Date: 14 July 1934
Birth Place: Sabraton, W.Va.
Death Date: 18 July 1934
Burial Date: 19 July 1934
Race: W
Gender: F
Cemetery: Monongalia County, W.V. Cemetery


Name: Frank Milich
Birth Date: Unknown
Birth Place: Unknown
Death Date: 17 November 1934
Burial Date: 26 November 1934
Race: W
Gender: M
Cemetery: Monongalia County, W.V. Cemetery


Name: Rosa Thomas
Birth Date: 23 December
Birth Place: Institute, W.Va.
Death Date: 23 October 1934
Burial Date: 28 October 1934
Race: C
Gender: F
Cemetery: Monongalia County, W.V. Cemetery

Name: Joe Patroski
Birth Date: Unknown
Birth Place: Poland
Death Date: 14 June 1934
Burial Date: 14 June 1934
Race: W
Gender: M
Cemetery: Monongalia County, W.V. Cemetery


Name: Henry Robinson
Birth Date: Unknown
Birth Place: Unknown
Death Date: 29 June 1934
Burial Date: 29 June 1934
Race: W
Gender: M
Cemetery: Monongalia County, W.V. Cemetery


Name: Nellie Runion
Birth Date: 01 June
Birth Place: Unknown
Death Date: 13 August 1934
Burial Date: 25 March 1935
Race: W
Gender: F
Cemetery: Monongalia County, W.V. Cemetery

Name: Peter Silbuski
Birth Date: Unknown
Birth Place: Poland
Death Date: 24 August 1934
Burial Date: 27 August 1934
Race: W
Gender: M
Cemetery: Monongalia County, W.V. Cemetery


Name: Wm Ward
Birth Date: Unknown
Birth Place: Unknown
Death Date: 13 February 1934
Burial Date: 14 February 1934
Race: C
Gender: M
Cemetery: Monongalia County, W.V. Cemetery


Name: James H. Wayson
Birth Date: Unknown
Birth Place: W.Va.
Death Date: 14 October 1934
Burial Date: 15 October 1934
Race: C
Gender: M
Cemetery: Monongalia County, W.V. Cemetery

Name: Sarah Bimbo Williams
Birth Date: Unknown
Birth Place: Alabama
Death Date: 15 January 1934
Burial Date: 20 January 1934
Race: C
Gender: F
Cemetery: Monongalia County, W.V. Cemetery

# 1935

Name: Robert Campbell
Birth Date: 24 January 1935
Birth Place: Allegheny County, Pa.
Death Date: 16 February 1935
Burial Date: 17 February 1935
Race: W
Gender: M
Cemetery: Monongalia County, W.V. Cemetery


Name: Joe Dorko
Birth Date: Unknown
Birth Place: Hungary
Death Date: 23 November 1935
Burial Date: 25 November 1935
Race: W
Gender: M
Cemetery: Monongalia County, W.V. Cemetery


Name:        Lewis Eiklo
Birth Date: 1876
Birth Place: Unknown
Death Date: 26 November 1935
Burial Date: 27 November 1935
Race: W
Gender: M
Cemetery: Monongalia County, W.V. Cemetery

Name: Flollie J. Estep
Birth Date: 16 July 1907
Birth Place: Randolph County, W.Va
Death Date: 12 November 1935
Burial Date: 13 November 1935
Race: W
Gender: F
Cemetery: Monongalia County, W.V. Cemetery


Name: William Farrell
Birth Date: Unknown
Birth Place: Unknown
Death Date: 15 December 1935
Burial Date: 16 December 1935
Race: W
Gender: M
Cemetery: Monongalia County, W.V. Cemetery


Name: Baby Boy Hardman
Birth Date: 22 February 1935
Birth Place: Almina, W.Va.
Death Date: 23 February 1935
Burial Date: 25 February 1935
Race: W
Gender: M
Cemetery: Monongalia County, W.V. Cemetery

Name: Carl Hart
Birth Date: Uknown
Birth Place: Unknown
Death Date: 17 July 1935
Burial Date: 19 July 1935
Race: W
Gender: M
Cemetery: Monongalia County, W.V. Cemetery


Name: William Hughes
Birth Date: Unknown
Birth Place: Unknown
Death Date: 02 November 1935
Burial Date: 04 November 1935
Race: W
Gender: M
Cemetery: Monongalia County, W.V. Cemetery


Name:Lasko Magor
Birth Date: Unknown
Birth Place: Poland
Death Date: 08 January 1935
Burial Date: 10 January 1935
Race: W
Gender: M
Cemetery: Monongalia County, W.V. Cemetery

Name: Steve Martin
Birth Date: Unknown
Birth Place: Russia
Death Date: 18 January 1935
Burial Date: 23 January 1935
Race: W
Gender: M
Cemetery: Monongalia County, W.V. Cemetery


Name: Everett Kahle
Birth Date: Unknown
Birth Place: Unknown
Death Date: 06 February 1935
Burial Date: 08 February 1935
Race: W
Gender: M
Cemetery: Monongalia County, W.V. Cemetery


Name: John Kammski
Birth Date: Unknown
Birth Place: Unknown
Death Date: 26 June 1935
Burial Date: 27 June1935
Race: W
Gender: M
Cemetery: Monongalia County, W.V. Cemetery

Name: Charles Kelley
Birth Date: Unknown
Birth Place: Unknown
Death Date: 08 December 1935
Burial Date: 11 December 1935
Race: C
Gender: M
Cemetery: Monongalia County, W.V. Cemetery


Name: John Kirby
Birth Date: Unknown
Birth Place: Unknown
Death Date: 09 July 1935
Burial Date: 10 July 1935
Race: C
Gender: M
Cemetery: Monongalia County, W.V. Cemetery


Name: Melliah Knisosky
Birth Date: Unknown
Birth Place: Austria
Death Date: 31 October 1935
Burial Date: 02 November 1935
Race: W
Gender: M
Cemetery: Monongalia County, W.V. Cemetery

Name: Wm. Parker
Birth Date: Unknown
Birth Place: St. George, Md.
Death Date: 07 July 1935
Burial Date: 09 July 1935
Race: W
Gender: M
Cemetery: Monongalia County, W.V. Cemetery


Name: James Redman
Birth Date: Unknown
Birth Place: North Carolina
Death Date: 06 January 1935
Burial Date: 08 January 1935
Race: C
Gender: M
Cemetery: Monongalia County, W.V. Cemetery


Name: Ted Schyp
Birth Date: Unknown
Birth Place: Unknown
Death Date: 28 January 1935
Burial Date: 30 January 1935
Race: W
Gender: M
Cemetery: Monongalia County, W.V. Cemetery

# 1936

Name:Steve Baboclesrich
Birth Date: Unknown
Birth Place: Unknown
Death Date: 08 May 1936
Burial Date: 15 May 1936
Race: W
Gender: M
Cemetery: Monongalia County, W.V. Cemetery


Name:Lowie Bichok
Birth Date: Unknown
Birth Place: Unknown
Death Date: 15 October 1936
Burial Date: 20 October 1936
Race: W
Gender: M
Cemetery: Monongalia County, W.V. Cemetery


Name:Wm. Bufford
Birth Date: Unknown
Birth Place: Unknown
Death Date: 02 December 1936
Burial Date: 03 December 1936
Race: C
Gender: M
Cemetery: Monongalia County, W.V. Cemetery

Name:John Cermac
Birth Date: Unknown
Birth Place: Unknown
Death Date: 27 July 1936
Burial Date: 30 July 1936
Race: W
Gender: M
Cemetery: Monongalia County, W.V. Cemetery


Name: John Dobos
Birth Date: Unknown
Birth Place: Austria Hungary
Death Date: 11 November 1936
Burial Date: 13 November 1936
Race: W
Gender: M
Cemetery: Monongalia County, W.V. Cemetery


Name:John Doycholc
Birth Date: 12 May 1875
Birth Place: Europe
Death Date: 05 May 1936
Burial Date: 05 May 1936
Race: W
Gender: M
Cemetery: Monongalia County, W.V. Cemetery

Name: Grace Fain
Birth Date: 29 March 1929
Birth Place: Liberty, W.Va.
Death Date: 25 February 1936
Burial Date: 29 February 1936
Race: C
Gender: F
Cemetery: Monongalia County, W.V. Cemetery


Name:Thomas Flesher
Birth Date: Unknown
Birth Place: Unknown
Death Date: 05 August 1936
Burial Date: 07 August 1936
Race: W
Gender: M
Cemetery: Monongalia County, W.V. Cemetery


Name:John Hydok
Birth Date: Unknown
Birth Place: Unknown
Death Date: 03 May 1936
Burial Date: 04 May 1936
Race: W
Gender: M
Cemetery: Monongalia County, W.V. Cemetery

Name:Jackson Lowers
Birth Date: Unknown
Birth Place: "Fayett City, Pa."
Death Date: 05 January 1936
Burial Date: 08 January 1936
Race:W
Gender: M
Cemetery: Monongalia County, W.V. Cemetery


Name:Joe Matach
Birth Date: Unknown
Birth Place: Unknown
Death Date: 09 March 1936
Burial Date: 14 March 1936
Race: W
Gender: M
Cemetery: Monongalia County, W.V. Cemetery


Name:Ella McDonald
Birth Date: Unknown
Birth Place: Unknown
Death Date: 01 June 1936
Burial Date: 02 June 1936
Race: W
Gender: F
Cemetery: Monongalia County, W.V. Cemetery

Name:John McGinley
Birth Date: Unknown
Birth Place: Pa.
Death Date: 28 June 1936
Burial Date: 01 July 1936
Race: W
Gender: M
Cemetery: Monongalia County, W.V. Cemetery


Name:George Polovina
Birth Date: Unknown
Birth Place: Unknown
Death Date: 13 March 1936
Burial Date: 14 March 1936
Race: W
Gender: M
Cemetery: Monongalia County, W.V. Cemetery


Name: Charley Rohozin
Birth Date: 24 May 1936
Birth Place: Sabraton, W.Va.
Death Date: 23 October 1936
Burial Date: 24 October 1936
Race: W
Gender: M
Cemetery: Monongalia County, W.V. Cemetery

Name:Alex Sechrome
Birth Date: Unknown
Birth Place: Russia
Death Date: 22 June 1936
Burial Date: 26 June 1936
Race: W
Gender: M
Cemetery: Monongalia County, W.V. Cemetery


Name:Franklin Rosevelt Sites
Birth Date: 18 April 1936
Birth Place: Maidsville, W.Va
Death Date: 25 April 1936
Burial Date: 27 April 1936
Race: W
Gender: M
Cemetery: Monongalia County, W.V. Cemetery


Name:John Stacker
Birth Date: 17 February 1868
Birth Place: Scotland
Death Date: 09 June 1936
Burial Date: 12 June 1936
Race: W
Gender: M
Cemetery: Monongalia County, W.V. Cemetery

Name:Joe Tath
Birth Date: Unknown
Birth Place: Hungary
Death Date: 02 July 1936
Burial Date: 05 July 1936
Race: W
Gender: M
Cemetery: Monongalia County, W.V. Cemetery


Name: Unknown
Birth Date: Unknown
Birth Place: Unknown
Death Date: 29 July 1936
Burial Date: 29 July 1936
Race: W
Gender: M
Cemetery: Monongalia County, W.V. Cemetery

# 1937

Name:George Abbott
Birth Date: 15 September 1872
Birth Place: Ohio
Death Date: 01 September 1937
Burial Date: 03 September 1937
Race: W
Gender: M
Cemetery: Monongalia County, W.V. Cemetery


Name: John Brago
Birth Date: Unknown
Birth Place: Austria
Death Date: 05 February 1937
Burial Date: 06 February 1937
Race: W
Gender: M
Cemetery: Monongalia County, W.V. Cemetery


Name: Joe Bedancourt
Birth Date: Unknown
Birth Place: Mexico
Death Date: 10 January 1937
Burial Date: 13 January 1937
Race: Mexican
Gender: M
Cemetery: Monongalia County, W.V. Cemetery

Name:Mike Begovich
Birth Date: Unknown
Birth Place: Austria
Death Date: 06 August 1937
Burial Date: 07 August 1937
Race: W
Gender: M
Cemetery: Monongalia County, W.V. Cemetery


Name: Mary E. Brown
Birth Date: 08 January 1897
Birth Place: Ala
Death Date: 04 March 1937
Burial Date: 08 March 1937
Race: C
Gender: F
Cemetery: Monongalia County, W.V. Cemetery


Name: James Clark
Birth Date: Unknown
Birth Place: Maryland
Death Date: 07 April 1937
Burial Date: 10 April 1937
Race: C
Gender:M
Cemetery: Monongalia County, W.V. Cemetery

Name: John H. Cline
Birth Date: 1869
Birth Place: Brownsville, Pennsylvania
Death Date: 25 July 1937
Burial Date: 27 July 1937
Race: W
Gender: M
Cemetery: Monongalia County, W.V. Cemetery


Name: Walter Franklin Crislip
Birth Date: 13 October 1936
Birth Place: Maidsville, W.Va
Death Date: 16 September 1937
Burial Date: 19 September 1937
Race: W
Gender: M
Cemetery: Monongalia County, W.V. Cemetery


Name:Harry Dawson
Birth Date: Unknown
Birth Place: California, Pa.
Death Date: 09 March 1937
Burial Date: 13 March 1937
Race: W
Gender: M
Cemetery: Monongalia County, W.V. Cemetery

Name: John Garrity
Birth Date: 24 February 1870
Birth Place: England
Death Date: 14 May 1937
Burial Date: 17 May 1937
Race: W
Gender: M
Cemetery: Monongalia County, W.V. Cemetery


Name:Barbara Ellen Glendening
Birth Date: Unknown
Birth Place: Jefferson County, W.Va
Death Date: 17 February 1937
Burial Date: 19 February 1937
Race: W
Gender: F
Cemetery: Monongalia County, W.V. Cemetery


Name:John Gray
Birth Date: About 1866
Birth Place: Unknown
Death Date: 11 April 1937
Burial Date: 14 April 1937
Race: W
Gender: M
Cemetery: Monongalia County, W.V. Cemetery

Name: Maggie Hampton
Birth Date: 15  March 1900
Birth Place: Martinsville
Death Date: 10 May 1937
Burial Date: 12 May 1937
Race: C
Gender: F
Cemetery: Monongalia County, W.V. Cemetery


Name:Yvonne Lee Hardman
Birth Date: 09 February 1937
Birth Place: Brady, W.Va.
Death Date: 22 February 1937
Burial Date: 23 February 1937
Race: W
Gender: F
Cemetery: Monongalia County, W.V. Cemetery


Name:Mike Herbetka
Birth Date: Unknown
Birth Place: Russia
Death Date: 12 August 1937
Burial Date: 13 August 1937
Race: W
Gender: M
Cemetery: Monongalia County, W.V. Cemetery

Name:Louise Hunter
Birth Date: March 1896
Birth Place: South Carolina
Death Date: 29 October 1937
Burial Date: 31 October 1937
Race: C
Gender:F
Cemetery: Monongalia County, W.V. Cemetery


Name: John Katlitnik
Birth Date: Unknown
Birth Place: Unknown
Death Date: 31 January 1937
Burial Date: 02 February 1937
Race: W
Gender: M
Cemetery: Monongalia County, W.V. Cemetery


Name: Thomas Kerns
Birth Date: Unknown
Birth Place: Ireland
Death Date: 31 January 1937
Burial Date: 02 February 1937
Race: W
Gender: M
Cemetery: Monongalia County, W.V. Cemetery

Name: Jacob Kotar
Birth Date: Unknown
Birth Place: Unknown
Death Date: 25 December 1937
Burial Date: 29 December 1937
Race: W
Gender: M
Cemetery: Monongalia County, W.V. Cemetery


Name: Joe Lozkos
Birth Date: Unknown
Birth Place: Hungary
Death Date: 24 May 1937
Burial Date: 28 May 1937
Race: W
Gender:M
Cemetery: Monongalia County, W.V. Cemetery


Name: Effie Mace
Birth Date: 26 July 1919
Birth Place: Gilmer County, W.Va
Death Date: 04 January 1937
Burial Date: 07 January 1937
Race: W
Gender: F
Cemetery: Monongalia County, W.V. Cemetery

Name: Joe Magyar
Birth Date: About 1877
Birth Place: Hungary
Death Date: 19 or 20 July 1937
Burial Date: 21 July 1937
Race: W
Gender: M
Cemetery: Monongalia County, W.V. Cemetery


Name: A. Carnell Mock
Birth Date: 07 January 1937
Birth Place: W.Va.
Death Date: 25 June 1937
Burial Date: 27 June 1937
Race: W
Gender: M
Cemetery: Monongalia County, W.V. Cemetery


Name: Stanley Morris
Birth Date: Unknown
Birth Place: W.Va/Poland
Death Date: 04 May 1937
Burial Date: 06 May 1937
Race: W
Gender: M
Cemetery: Monongalia County, W.V. Cemetery

Name:John Oshouski
Birth Date: 15 January 1865
Birth Place: Unknown
Death Date: 20 September 1937
Burial Date: 21 September 1937
Race: W
Gender: M
Cemetery: Monongalia County, W.V. Cemetery


Name: Dute Parson
Birth Date: Unknown
Birth Place: Ala
Death Date: 26 June 1937
Burial Date: 29 June 1937
Race: C
Gender: M
Cemetery: Monongalia County, W.V. Cemetery


Name: Frank Sarkos
Birth Date: Unknown
Birth Place: Hungary
Death Date: 02 January 1937
Burial Date: 05 January 1937
Race: W
Gender: M
Cemetery: Monongalia County, W.V. Cemetery

Name: Rachel Elizabeth Stalker
Birth Date: 20 October 1874
Birth Place: Preston County, W.Va.
Death Date: 25 October 1937
Burial Date: 27 October 1937
Race: W
Gender: F
Cemetery: Monongalia County, W.V. Cemetery


Name:Joseph Teth
Birth Date: 1868
Birth Place: Austria, Hungary
Death Date: 04 October 1937
Burial Date: 06 October 1937
Race: W
Gender: M
Cemetery: Monongalia County, W.V. Cemetery


Name: Charles Wilson
Birth Date: 22 July 1898
Birth Place: N.C.
Death Date: 16 September 1937
Burial Date: 19 September 1937
Race: W
Gender: M
Cemetery: Monongalia County, W.V. Cemetery

Name: George Zanoz
Birth Date: Unknown
Birth Place: Unknown
Death Date: 07 January 1937
Burial Date: 09 January 1937
Race: W
Gender: M
Cemetery: Monongalia County, W.V. Cemetery

# 1938

Name: Wm. Bunting
Birth Date: 14 August 1862
Birth Place: England
Death Date: 24 May 1938
Burial Date: 25 May 1938
Race: W
Gender: M
Cemetery: Monongalia County, W.V. Cemetery

Name: Tony Burselo
Birth Date: Unknown
Birth Place: Austria
Death Date: 22 March 1938
Burial Date: 24 March 1938
Race: W
Gender: M
Cemetery: Monongalia County, W.V. Cemetery

Name: Ellis Caldwell
Birth Date: 09 April 1865
Birth Place: Ala
Death Date: 01 April 1938
Burial Date: 04 April 1938
Race: C
Gender: M
Cemetery: Monongalia County, W.V. Cemetery

Name: Cordelia Ann Clauston
Birth Date: 1855
Birth Place: Randolph County, W.Va.
Death Date: 23 September 1938
Burial Date: 24 September 1938
Race: W
Gender: F
Cemetery: Monongalia County, W.V. Cemetery


Name: Frank Cody
Birth Date: 15 December 1880
Birth Place: Greensborro, Alabama
Death Date: About 25 May 1938
Burial Date: 27 May 1938
Race: C
Gender: M
Cemetery: Monongalia County, W.V. Cemetery


Name: Edward Ellis Green
Birth Date: 10 September 1869
Birth Place: Powhatan, Ohio
Death Date: 03 January 1938
Burial Date: 05 January 1938
Race: W
Gender: M
Cemetery: Monongalia County, W.V. Cemetery

Name: Russell Hall
Birth Date: 29 July 1938
Birth Place: Sabraton, W.Va
Death Date: 10 October 1938
Burial Date: 11 October 1938
Race: W
Gender: M
Cemetery: Monongalia County, W.V. Cemetery


Name: Margaret Elizabeth Hanford
Birth Date: 30 December 1936
Birth Place: Morgantown, W.Va.
Death Date: 02 November 1938
Burial Date: 04 November 1938
Race: W
Gender: F
Cemetery: Monongalia County, W.V. Cemetery


Name: Louis Konach
Birth Date: Unknown
Birth Place: Hungary
Death Date: 01 October 1938
Burial Date: 03 October 1938
Race: W
Gender: M
Cemetery: Monongalia County, W.V. Cemetery

Name: Michael Joseph O'Malley
Birth Date: 01 January 1875
Birth Place: Maryland
Death Date: 25 October 1938
Burial Date: 26 October 1938
Race: W
Gender: M
Cemetery: Monongalia County, W.V. Cemetery


Name: Felix Porpun
Birth Date: 02 March 1891
Birth Place: Russia
Death Date: 07 July 1938
Burial Date: 08 July 1938
Race: W
Gender: M
Cemetery: Monongalia County, W.V. Cemetery


Name: William ... Riley
Birth Date: 09 August 1896
Birth Place: Newburg, W.Va.
Death Date: 10 June 1938
Burial Date: 12 June 1938
Race: W
Gender: M
Cemetery: Monongalia County, W.V. Cemetery

Name: Tony Ritz
Birth Date: 1866
Birth Place: Hungary
Death Date: 07 August 1938
Burial Date: 08 August 1938
Race: W
Gender: M
Cemetery: Monongalia County, W.V. Cemetery


Name: Ella Seabrick
Birth Date: Unknown
Birth Place: Unknown
Death Date: 02 March 1938
Burial Date: 11 March 1938
Race: W
Gender: F
Cemetery: Monongalia County, W.V. Cemetery


Name: John Subak
Birth Date: Unknown
Birth Place: Europe/Croatian
Death Date: 10 November 1938
Burial Date: 14 November 1938
Race: W
Gender: M
Cemetery: Monongalia County, W.V. Cemetery

Name: Tony Tiuk
Birth Date: Unknown
Birth Place: Austria
Death Date: 05 May 1938
Burial Date: 09 May 1938
Race: W
Gender: W
Cemetery: Monongalia County, W.V. Cemetery


Name: Charles Yencobinas
Birth Date: Unknown
Birth Place: Unknown
Death Date: 29 December 1938
Burial Date: 31 December 1938
Race: W
Gender: M
Cemetery: Monongalia County, W.V. Cemetery


Name: Tony Zinco
Birth Date: Unknown
Birth Place: Unknown
Death Date: 21 September 1938
Burial Date: 24 September 1938
Race: W
Gender: M
Cemetery: Monongalia County, W.V. Cemetery

# 1939

Name: Eugene Archer
Birth Date: 21 January 1861
Birth Place: W.Va.
Death Date: 25 May 1939
Burial Date: 26 May 1939
Race: W
Gender: M
Cemetery: Monongalia County, W.V. Cemetery


Name: Mary Arnold
Birth Date: 06 May 1939
Birth Place: W.Va.
Death Date: 17 May 1939
Burial Date: 17 May 1939
Race: C
Gender: F
Cemetery: Monongalia County, W.V. Cemetery


Name: Joseph Boogher
Birth Date: 09 August 1878
Birth Place: W.Va.
Death Date: 09 June 1939
Burial Date: 13 June 1939
Race: W
Gender: M
Cemetery: Monongalia County, W.V. Cemetery

Name: George Burgess
Birth Date: 05 October 1869
Birth Place: Pennsylvania
Death Date: 29 January 1939
Burial Date: 31 January 1939
Race: W
Gender: M
Cemetery: Monongalia County, W.V. Cemetery


Name: James W. Campbell
Birth Date: Unknown
Birth Place: Elizabeth, Pa.
Death Date: 19 July 1939
Burial Date: 22 July 1939
Race: W
Gender: M
Cemetery: Monongalia County, W.V. Cemetery


Name: Paul Charnow
Birth Date: 12 July 1895
Birth Place: Russia
Death Date: 19 June 1939
Burial Date: 21 June 1939
Race: W
Gender: M
Cemetery: Monongalia County, W.V. Cemetery

Name: Fred Datzuk
Birth Date: Unknown
Birth Place: Russia
Death Date: 21 February 1939
Burial Date: 22 February 1939
Race: W
Gender: M
Cemetery: Monongalia County, W.V. Cemetery


Name: Andy Fordor
Birth Date: Unknown
Birth Place: Finland
Death Date: 15 May 1939
Burial Date: 18 May 1939
Race: W
Gender: M
Cemetery: Monongalia County, W.V. Cemetery


Name: Bruno Galaski
Birth Date: 18 December 1877
Birth Place: Poland
Death Date: 25 January 1939
Burial Date: 26 January 1939
Race: W
Gender: M
Cemetery: Monongalia County, W.V. Cemetery

Name: Tony Gebbes
Birth Date: 13 June 1883
Birth Place: Russia
Death Date: 01 December 1939
Burial Date: 02 December 1939
Race: W
Gender: M
Cemetery: Monongalia County, W.V. Cemetery


Name: Frank Gump
Birth Date: 15 November 1853
Birth Place: Mt. Morris, Pennsylvania
Death Date: 21 January 1939
Burial Date: 22 January 1939
Race: W
Gender: M
Cemetery: Monongalia County, W.V. Cemetery


Name: Danial Jackson
Birth Date: 25 December 1885
Birth Place: Unknown
Death Date: 30 November 1939
Burial Date: 01 December 1939
Race: Black
Gender: M
Cemetery: Monongalia County, W.V. Cemetery

Name: Samuel P Johnson
Birth Date: 15 February 1863
Birth Place: Gladesville, W.Va.
Death Date: 30 April 1939
Burial Date: 01 May 1939
Race: W
Gender: M
Cemetery: Monongalia County, W.V. Cemetery


Name: Will Jones
Birth Date: Unknown
Birth Place: Tennesse
Death Date: 18 April 1939
Burial Date: 19 April 1939
Race: C
Gender: M
Cemetery: Monongalia County, W.V. Cemetery


Name: John Kotia
Birth Date: 1869
Birth Place: Hungary
Death Date: 19 January 1939
Burial Date: 20 January 1939
Race: W
Gender: M
Cemetery: Monongalia County, W.V. Cemetery

Name: Alex Kovach
Birth Date: about 1887
Birth Place: Unknown
Death Date: 12 March 1939
Burial Date: 14 March 1939
Race: W
Gender:M
Cemetery: Monongalia County, W.V. Cemetery


Name: Joe Kurche
Birth Date: Unknown
Birth Place: Hungary
Death Date: 20 March 1939
Burial Date: 21 March 1939
Race: W
Gender:M
Cemetery: Monongalia County, W.V. Cemetery


Name: Roy Allen Lipscomb
Birth Date: 02 September 1939
Birth Place: Monongalia County, W.Va
Death Date: 02 September 1939
Burial Date: 05 September 1939
Race: W
Gender: M
Cemetery: Monongalia County, W.V. Cemetery

Name: John Mayse
Birth Date: 28 June 1862
Birth Place: Lewis County, W.Va.
Death Date: 22 September 1939
Burial Date: 23 September 1939
Race: W
Gender: M
Cemetery: Monongalia County, W.V. Cemetery


Name: Helen Marie McGilton
Birth Date: 11 June 1937
Birth Place: Monongalia County, W.Va.
Death Date: 27 February 1939
Burial Date: 01 March 1939
Race: W
Gender:F
Cemetery: Monongalia County, W.V. Cemetery


Name: Rebecca McGinley
Birth Date: 1856
Birth Place: Pennsylvania
Death Date: 22 November 1939
Burial Date: 25 November 1939
Race: W
Gender:F
Cemetery: Monongalia County, W.V. Cemetery

Name: Ruth Murphy
Birth Date: 09 September 1939
Birth Place: Morgantown, W.Va.
Death Date: 30 November 1939
Burial Date: 04 December 1939
Race: W
Gender: F
Cemetery: Monongalia County, W.V. Cemetery


Name: Joseph Musick
Birth Date: Unknown
Birth Place: Poland
Death Date: 10 July 1939
Burial Date: 12 July 1939
Race: W
Gender: M
Cemetery: Monongalia County, W.V. Cemetery


Name: Charles Myrick
Birth Date: Unknown
Birth Place: Alabama
Death Date: 02 June 1939
Burial Date: 08 June 1939
Race: C
Gender: M
Cemetery: Monongalia County, W.V. Cemetery

Name: Pete Precupis
Birth Date: Unknown
Birth Place: Romania
Death Date: 28 January 1939
Burial Date: 29 January 1939
Race: W
Gender: M
Cemetery: Monongalia County, W.V. Cemetery


Name: David Ramsey
Birth Date: 13 April 1849
Birth Place: Pa.
Death Date: 09 January 1939
Burial Date: 11 January 1939
Race: W
Gender: M
Cemetery: Monongalia County, W.V. Cemetery


Name: John Rasnick
Birth Date: Unknown
Birth Place: Russia
Death Date: 18 April 1939
Burial Date: 18 April 1939
Race: W
Gender: M
Cemetery: Monongalia County, W.V. Cemetery

Name: George Kenneth Riffle
Birth Date: 01 March 1939
Birth Place: Morgantown, W.Va.
Death Date: 22 March 1939
Burial Date: 23 March 1939
Race: W
Gender: M
Cemetery: Monongalia County, W.V. Cemetery


Name: Andy Smith
Birth Date: 17 August 1875
Birth Place: Lithuania
Death Date: 01 January 1939
Burial Date: 03 January 1939
Race: W
Gender: M
Cemetery: Monongalia County, W.V. Cemetery


Name: Theresa Szency
Birth Date: 1868
Birth Place: Austria Hungary
Death Date: 18 November 1939
Burial Date: 20 November 1939
Race: W
Gender: M
Cemetery: Monongalia County, W.V. Cemetery

Name: Willie Tucker
Birth Date: 25 December 1900
Birth Place: Durant, Tennessee
Death Date: 31 March 1939
Burial Date: 03 April 1939
Race: Negro
Gender:  M
Cemetery: Monongalia County, W.V. Cemetery


Name: Mike Vasiloff
Birth Date: Uknown
Birth Place: Bulgaria
Death Date: 30 March 1939
Burial Date: 31 March 1939
Race: W
Gender: M
Cemetery: Monongalia County, W.V. Cemetery


Name: Grucian Ziro
Birth Date: 16 November 1882
Birth Place: Austria Hungary
Death Date: 30 August 1939
Burial Date: 01 September 1939
Race: W
Gender: M
Cemetery: Monongalia County, W.V. Cemetery

# 1940

Name: Mike Manos
Birth Date: Unknown
Birth Place:Unknown
Death Date: 21 March 1940
Burial Date: 23 March 1940
Race: W
Gender: M
Cemetery: Monongalia County, W.V. Cemetery


Name: Alex Rogaski
Birth Date:about 1873
Birth Place: Poland
Death Date: 05 March 1940
Burial Date: 08 March 1940
Race: W
Gender: M
Cemetery: Monongalia County, W.V. Cemetery


Name: Joseph Tassick
Birth Date:Unknown
Birth Place:Austria
Death Date: 22 March 1940
Burial Date: 23 March 1940
Race: W
Gender:M
Cemetery: Monongalia County, W.V. Cemetery

Name: William Jennings Gargan
Birth Date: 09 December 1899
Birth Place: Fayette City, W.Va.
Death Date: 27 January 1940
Burial Date: 30 January 1940
Race: W
Gender:M
Cemetery: Monongalia County, W.V. Cemetery


Name: Nick Bezo
Birth Date:Unknown
Birth Place: Unknown
Death Date: 05 April 1940
Burial Date: 08 April 1940
Race: W
Gender:M
Cemetery: Monongalia County, W.V. Cemetery


Name: Tony Brosky
Birth Date:18 June 1883
Birth Place: Poland
Death Date: 04 April 1940
Burial Date: 06 April 1940
Race: W
Gender:M
Cemetery: Monongalia County, W.V. Cemetery

Name: Robert Jones
Birth Date: 18 September 1895
Birth Place: Alabama
Death Date: 04 March 1940
Burial Date: 08 March 1940
Race: Negro
Gender: M
Cemetery: Monongalia County, W.V. Cemetery


Name: William Brosack
Birth Date: 03 June 1870
Birth Place: Lithuania
Death Date: 07 May 1940
Burial Date: 09 May 1940
Race: W
Gender:M
Cemetery: Monongalia County, W.V. Cemetery


Name: William Mitchell
Birth Date: 1874
Birth Place: Lithuania
Death Date: 15 May 1940
Burial Date: 17 May 1940
Race: W
Gender: W
Cemetery: Monongalia County, W.V. Cemetery

Name: Kosto or George Yates Pronto
Birth Date: Unknown
Birth Place: Unknown
Death Date: 09 May 1940
Burial Date: 11 May 1940
Race: W
Gender: M
Cemetery: Monongalia County, W.V. Cemetery


Name: John Brkich
Birth Date: 03 February 1882
Birth Place: Jugo Slavia
Death Date: 02 June 1940
Burial Date: 04 June 1940
Race: W
Gender: M
Cemetery: Monongalia County, W.V. Cemetery


Name: John Smith
Birth Date: Unknown
Birth Place: Philadelphia, Pa.
Death Date: 19 June 1940
Burial Date: 19 June 1940
Race: C
Gender:M
Cemetery: Monongalia County, W.V. Cemetery

Name: John Shanks
Birth Date: about 1868
Birth Place: Chambersburg, Pa.
Death Date: 28 August 1940
Burial Date: 30 August 1940
Race: W
Gender: M
Cemetery: Monongalia County, W.V. Cemetery


Name: Mike Popovich
Birth Date:Unknown
Birth Place: Unknown
Death Date: 12 September 1940
Burial Date: 12 September 1940
Race: W
Gender: M
Cemetery: Monongalia County, W.V. Cemetery


Name: Johnathan Wright
Birth Date:05 December 1960
Birth Place: Monongalia County, W.Va.
Death Date: 01 October 1940
Burial Date: 03 October 1940
Race: W
Gender: M
Cemetery: Monongalia County, W.V. Cemetery

Name: Helen Louise McClead
Birth Date: 12 July 1940
Birth Place: Star City, W.Va.
Death Date: 23 November 1940
Burial Date: 25 November 1940
Race: W
Gender: F
Cemetery: Monongalia County, W.V. Cemetery


Name: Samuel R. Merrill
Birth Date: 15 November 1865
Birth Place: Wetzel County, W.Va.
Death Date: 24 November 1940
Burial Date: 26 November 1940
Race: W
Gender: M
Cemetery: Monongalia County, W.V. Cemetery


Name: Joseph Szoke
Birth Date: 18 March 1878
Birth Place: Austria
Death Date: 06 December 1940
Burial Date: 07 December 1940
Race: W
Gender: M
Cemetery: Monongalia County, W.V. Cemetery

Name: John Corbin
Birth Date: 06 July 1866
Birth Place: Thomas, W.Va.
Death Date: 12 January 1940
Burial Date: 16 January 1940
Race: W
Gender: M
Cemetery: Monongalia County, W.V. Cemetery


Name: Walter Stephens
Birth Date: 04 December 1900
Birth Place: Long View, Texas
Death Date: 26 January 1940
Burial Date: 29 January 1940
Race: Black
Gender: M
Cemetery: Monongalia County, W.V. Cemetery


Name: Mike Zevidor
Birth Date: 18 January 1877
Birth Place: Jugo Slavia
Death Date: 18 January 1940
Burial Date: 19 January 1940
Race: W
Gender:M
Cemetery: Monongalia County, W.V. Cemetery

Name: Freddie Jackson
Birth Date: 1939
Birth Place: W.Va.
Death Date: 16 February 1940
Burial Date: 17 February 1940
Race: W
Gender: M
Cemetery: Monongalia County, W.V. Cemetery


Name: Shirley Roberta Nuzum
Birth Date: 16 September 1938
Birth Place: Sycamore, Pa.
Death Date: 17 February 1940
Burial Date: 21 February 1940
Race: W
Gender: F
Cemetery: Monongalia County, W.V. Cemetery


Name: Martin Luther Stockwell
Birth Date: 29 July 1866
Birth Place: W.Va.
Death Date: 21 February 1940
Burial Date: 24 February 1940
Race: W
Gender: M
Cemetery: Monongalia County, W.V. Cemetery

# 1941

Name: William Henry Barnes
Birth Date: 07 June 1865
Birth Place: Maidsville, Monongalia County, W.Va.
Death Date: 29 June 1941
Burial Date: 30 June 1941
Race: W
Gender: M
Cemetery: Monongalia County, W.V. Cemetery


Name: Martin Luther Beckner
Birth Date: 03 October 1871
Birth Place: Gilmer County, W.Va.
Death Date: 11 April 1941
Burial Date: 13 April 1941
Race: W
Gender: M
Cemetery: Monongalia County, W.V. Cemetery


Name: Leo Blasco
Birth Date: Unknown
Birth Place: "Czechslovia"
Death Date: 25 February 1941
Burial Date: 28 February 1941
Race: W
Gender: M
Cemetery: Monongalia County, W.V. Cemetery

Name: William Buriell
Birth Date: 15 March
Birth Place: Norfolk, Va.
Death Date: 24 July 1941
Burial Date: 25 July 1941
Race: C
Gender: M
Cemetery: Monongalia County, W.V. Cemetery


Name: Albert Crosley
Birth Date: 04 March 1882
Birth Place: Shelby County, Tenn.
Death Date: 12 December 1941
Burial Date: 14 December 1941
Race: C
Gender:M
Cemetery: Monongalia County, W.V. Cemetery


Name: Ignatz Dastral
Birth Date: 15 January 1867
Birth Place: Hungary
Death Date: 16 January 1941
Burial Date: 18 January 1941
Race: W
Gender: M
Cemetery: Monongalia County, W.V. Cemetery

Name: Roda May Fink
Birth Date: 15 May 1917
Birth Place:Gilmer County, W.Va.
Death Date: 09 April 1941
Burial Date: 11 April 1941
Race: W
Gender: F
Cemetery: Monongalia County, W.V. Cemetery


Name: Henry Gains
Birth Date: 19 September 1870
Birth Place: Ala.
Death Date: 02 December 1941
Burial Date: 03 December 1941
Race: C
Gender: M
Cemetery: Monongalia County, W.V. Cemetery


Name: Alex Gotso
Birth Date: 15 June 1877
Birth Place: Russia
Death Date: 02 July 1941
Burial Date: 02 July 1941
Race: W
Gender: M
Cemetery: Monongalia County, W.V. Cemetery

Name: Carl Hovatter
Birth Date: 17 January 1941
Birth Place: 112 Hough St. Morgantown, W.Va.
Death Date: 18 January 1941
Burial Date: 20 January 1941
Race: W
Gender: M
Cemetery: Monongalia County, W.V. Cemetery


Name: Guiseppe Ielasi
Birth Date: 10 December 1874
Birth Place: Italy
Death Date: 09 October 1941
Burial Date: 11 October 1941
Race: W
Gender: M
Cemetery: Monongalia County, W.V. Cemetery


Name: Alex Johnson
Birth Date: 21 July 1875
Birth Place: Danville, Va.
Death Date: 19 February 1941
Burial Date: 22 February 1941
Race: C
Gender: M
Cemetery: Monongalia County, W.V. Cemetery

Name: Alex Lantz
Birth Date: June 1860
Birth Place: Greene County, Pa.
Death Date: 07 December 1941
Burial Date: 09 December 1941
Race: W
Gender: M
Cemetery: Monongalia County, W.V. Cemetery


Name: George Lawliss
Birth Date: 10 June 1868
Birth Place: Cassville, W.Va.
Death Date: 12 May 1941
Burial Date: 13 May 1941
Race: W
Gender: M
Cemetery: Monongalia County, W.V. Cemetery


Name: Mary Madich
Birth Date: 11 January 1871
Birth Place: "Juyslavia"
Death Date: 14 June 1941
Burial Date: 14 June 1941
Race: W
Gender: F
Cemetery: Monongalia County, W.V. Cemetery

Name: Maggie McNeil
Birth Date: 08 July 1896
Birth Place: Louisa, Ky.
Death Date: 07 February 1941
Burial Date: 09 February 1941
Race: C
Gender: F
Cemetery: Monongalia County, W.V. Cemetery


Name: Donald Lee Myers
Birth Date: 29 October 1941
Birth Place: Canyon, Monongalia County, W.Va.
Death Date: 02 November 1941
Burial Date: 02 November 1941
Race: W
Gender: M
Cemetery: Monongalia County, W.V. Cemetery


Name: Robert Lee Myers
Birth Date: 19 October 1941
Birth Place: Canyon, Monongalia County, W.Va
Death Date: 30 October 1941
Burial Date: 02 November 1941
Race: W
Gender: M
Cemetery: Monongalia County, W.V. Cemetery

Name: Pete Nicolosh
Birth Date: 13 August 1882
Birth Place: Austria
Death Date: 09 December 1941
Burial Date: 10 December 1941
Race: W
Gender: M
Cemetery: Monongalia County, W.V. Cemetery


Name: Pete Parnash
Birth Date: 29 June 1879
Birth Place: Russia
Death Date: 29 January 1941
Burial Date: 31 January 1941
Race: W
Gender: M
Cemetery: Monongalia County, W.V. Cemetery


Name: John Thomas Simmons
Birth Date: 12 January 1864
Birth Place: Pittsburg, Pa.
Death Date: 29 September 1941
Burial Date: 01 October 1941
Race: W
Gender: M
Cemetery: Monongalia County, W.V. Cemetery

Name: Isaac Neuton Strosnider
Birth Date: 04 May 1872
Birth Place: Whetsel, County, W.Va.
Death Date: 14 January 1941
Burial Date: 16 January 1941
Race: W
Gender: M
Cemetery: Monongalia County, W.V. Cemetery


Name: Andrew Summerville
Birth Date: 17 October 1869
Birth Place: Snowshoe, Pa.
Death Date: 18 November 1941
Burial Date: 21 November 1941
Race: W
Gender: M
Cemetery: Monongalia County, W.V. Cemetery


Name: Lawrence Eugene Trickett
Birth Date: 15 June 1941
Birth Place: Jerome Park, Morgantown, W.Va.
Death Date: 28 July 1941
Burial Date: 29 July 1941
Race: W
Gender: M
Cemetery: Monongalia County, W.V. Cemetery

Name: Chas. Vodish
Birth Date: 14 December 1888
Birth Place: "Checo Slovikia"
Death Date: 24 December 1941
Burial Date: 27 December 1941
Race: W
Gender: M
Cemetery: Monongalia County, W.V. Cemetery


Name: Charles White
Birth Date: 09 May 1871
Birth Place: Andersen County, Tenn.
Death Date: 22 June 1941
Burial Date: 25 June 1941
Race: W
Gender: M
Cemetery: Monongalia County, W.V. Cemetery

# 1942

Name: Cecelia Ann Badencourt
Birth Date: 17 January 1942
Birth Place: W.Va.
Death Date: 16 April 1942
Burial Date: 17 April 1942
Race: W
Gender: F
Cemetery: Monongalia County, W.V. Cemetery


Name: John Bator
Birth Date: 06 August 1874
Birth Place: Poland
Death Date: 29 October 1942
Burial Date: 30 October 1942
Race: W
Gender: M
Cemetery: Monongalia County, W.V. Cemetery


Name: Joe Biggard
Birth Date: 03 January 1858
Birth Place: Pittsburgh, Pa.
Death Date: 01 December 1942
Burial Date: 01 December 1942
Race: W
Gender: M
Cemetery: Monongalia County, W.V. Cemetery

Name: Andy Borsuck
Birth Date: 21 August 1872
Birth Place: Russia
Death Date: 23 December 1942
Burial Date: 27 December 1942
Race: W
Gender: M
Cemetery: Monongalia County, W.V. Cemetery


Name: William Gilbert Creslip
Birth Date: 21 September 1941
Birth Place: Monongalia County, W.Va.
Death Date: 22 October 1942
Burial Date: 23 October 1942
Race: W
Gender: M
Cemetery: Monongalia County, W.V. Cemetery


Name: Frederick Gould
Birth Date: 19 September 1877
Birth Place: Marion County, W.Va.
Death Date: 03 November 1942
Burial Date: ----
Race: W
Gender: M
Cemetery: Monongalia County, W.V. Cemetery

Name: David R. Gwillen
Birth Date: 12 May 1859
Birth Place: Beaufort Wales
Death Date: 15 October 1942
Burial Date: 16 October 1942
Race: W
Gender: M
Cemetery: Monongalia County, W.V. Cemetery


Name: John Herbetko
Birth Date: 10 July 1866
Birth Place: Poland
Death Date: 07 September 1942
Burial Date: 08 September 1942
Race: W
Gender: M
Cemetery: Monongalia County, W.V. Cemetery


Name: Thomas Johnson
Birth Date: 01 July 1879
Birth Place: Georgia
Death Date: 12 April 1942
Burial Date: 14 April 1942
Race: C
Gender: M
Cemetery: Monongalia County, W.V. Cemetery

Name: Luciella Jones
Birth Date: 10 January 1892
Birth Place: Unknown
Death Date: 02 October 1942
Burial Date: 04 October 1942
Race: C
Gender: F
Cemetery: Monongalia County, W.V. Cemetery


Name: Loyal Thomas Lease
Birth Date: 20 July 1921
Birth Place: Maryland
Death Date: 06 December 1942
Burial Date: 08 December 1942
Race: W
Gender: M
Cemetery: Monongalia County, W.V. Cemetery


Name: Frank Lucy
Birth Date: Unknown
Birth Place: Unknown
Death Date: 06 January 1942
Burial Date: 15 January 1942
Race: W
Gender:M
Cemetery: Monongalia County, W.V. Cemetery

Name: Charlie Marshall
Birth Date: Unknown
Birth Place: Alabama
Death Date: 11 November 1942
Burial Date: 12 November 1942
Race: C
Gender: M
Cemetery: Monongalia County, W.V. Cemetery


Name: Steve Meuak
Birth Date: Unknown
Birth Place: Unknown
Death Date: 18 May 1942
Burial Date: 19 May 1942
Race: W
Gender: M
Cemetery: Monongalia County, W.V. Cemetery


Name: George Menak
Birth Date: 10 March 1866
Birth Place: Poland
Death Date: 09 October 1942
Burial Date: 12 October 1942
Race: W
Gender: M
Cemetery: Monongalia County, W.V. Cemetery

Name: John F. Novak
Birth Date: 04 April 1874
Birth Place: "Checo- Slovakia"
Death Date: 02 March 1942
Burial Date: 06 March 1942
Race: W
Gender: M
Cemetery: Monongalia County, W.V. Cemetery


Name: John Pavalich
Birth Date: 01 July 1859
Birth Place: Poland
Death Date: 15 January 1942
Burial Date: 16 January 1942
Race: W
Gender: M
Cemetery: Monongalia County, W.V. Cemetery


Name: Edward Pazel
Birth Date: Unknown
Birth Place: Russia
Death Date: 30 September 1942
Burial Date: ----
Race: W
Gender: M
Cemetery: Monongalia County, W.V. Cemetery

Name: Leonard Skeurtevich
Birth Date: Unknown
Birth Place: Unknown
Death Date: 16 March 1942
Burial Date: 19 March 1942
Race: W
Gender: M
Cemetery: Monongalia County, W.V. Cemetery


Name: Dominic Slivico
Birth Date: 04 August 1875
Birth Place: Czechoslovia
Death Date: 02 October 1942
Burial Date: 04 October 1942
Race: W
Gender: M
Cemetery: Monongalia County, W.V. Cemetery


Name: Paul Stass
Birth Date: 1874
Birth Place: "Checo-Slovakia"
Death Date: 07 January 1942
Burial Date: 09 January 1942
Race: W
Gender: M
Cemetery: Monongalia County, W.V. Cemetery

Name: George Stone
Birth Date: 15 September 1865
Birth Place: Unknown
Death Date: 09 October 1942
Burial Date: 12 October 1942
Race: W
Gender: M
Cemetery: Monongalia County, W.V. Cemetery


Name: Mahala Weaver
Birth Date: 23 February 1870
Birth Place: W.Va.
Death Date: 02 May 1942
Burial Date: 05 May 1942
Race: W
Gender: F
Cemetery: Monongalia County, W.V. Cemetery

# 1943

Name: Merril Echols
Birth Date: 20 November 1912
Birth Place: Rome, Georgia
Death Date: 07 March 1943
Burial Date: 11 March 1943
Race: Black
Gender: M
Cemetery: Monongalia County, W.V. Cemetery


Name: Joe Plovik
Birth Date: 20 March 1863
Birth Place: Czechoslovakia
Death Date: 20 March 1943
Burial Date: 23 March 1943
Race: W
Gender: M
Cemetery: Monongalia County, W.V. Cemetery


Name: James N. Brooks
Birth Date: 23 May 1886
Birth Place: Nashville, Tenn.
Death Date: 25 February 1943
Burial Date: 27 February 1943
Race: Col
Gender: M
Cemetery: Monongalia County, W.V. Cemetery

Name: Stanley Kurploski
Birth Date: 1887
Birth Place: Poland
Death Date: 01 February 1943
Burial Date: 03 February 1943
Race: W
Gender: M
Cemetery: Monongalia County, W.V. Cemetery


Name: Frank Paulus
Birth Date: 02 February 1878
Birth Place: Poland
Death Date: 16 February 1943
Burial Date: 19 February 1943
Race: W
Gender: M
Cemetery: Monongalia County, W.V. Cemetery


Name: John Paulus
Birth Date: 24 June 1862
Birth Place: poland
Death Date: 12 February 1943
Burial Date: 13 February 1943
Race: W
Gender: M
Cemetery: Monongalia County, W.V. Cemetery

Name: Paul Kohot
Birth Date: 18 August 1883
Birth Place: Poland
Death Date: 02 April 1943
Burial Date:  April 1943
Race: W
Gender: M
Cemetery: Monongalia County, W.V. Cemetery


Name: Chester Russell
Birth Date: 08 May 1864
Birth Place: Holland
Death Date: 04 April 1943
Burial Date: 07 April 1943
Race: W
Gender:  M
Cemetery: Monongalia County, W.V. Cemetery


Name: Victor Trotsky
Birth Date: April 1864
Birth Place: Russia
Death Date: 30 March 1943
Burial Date: 31 March 1943
Race: W
Gender:  M
Cemetery: Monongalia County, W.V. Cemetery

Name: Louis Kovach
Birth Date: 1888
Birth Place: Hungaria
Death Date: 10 May 1943
Burial Date: 14 May 1943
Race: W
Gender: M
Cemetery: Monongalia County, W.V. Cemetery


Name: George Hummell
Birth Date: 1862
Birth Place: Cambridge, Pa.
Death Date: 19 July 1943
Burial Date: 20 July 1943
Race: W
Gender: M
Cemetery: Monongalia County, W.V. Cemetery


Name: Joseph Marsh
Birth Date: 22 January 1884
Birth Place: Pagebank, England
Death Date: 12 February 1943
Burial Date: 16 February 1943
Race: W
Gender: M
Cemetery: Monongalia County, W.V. Cemetery

Name: Charles Minerd
Birth Date: Unknown
Birth Place: West Virginia
Death Date: 29 December 1943
Burial Date: 01 January 1944
Race: W
Gender: M
Cemetery: Monongalia County, W.V. Cemetery


Name: Frank Sluvak
Birth Date: Unknown
Birth Place: Austria
Death Date: 31 December 1943
Burial Date: 03 January 1944
Race: W
Gender: M
Cemetery: Monongalia County, W.V. Cemetery


Name: Adam Redesky
Birth Date: Unknown
Birth Place: Russia
Death Date: 06 December 1943
Burial Date: December 1943
Race: W
Gender: M
Cemetery: Monongalia County, W.V. Cemetery

# 1944

Name: Charles Asberry
Birth Date: 29 August 1856
Birth Place: Virginia
Death Date: 05 January 1944
Burial Date: 07 January 1944
Race: N
Gender: M
Cemetery: Monongalia County, W.V. Cemetery

Name: George Brazeten
Birth Date: 23 December 1880
Birth Place: Europe
Death Date: 19 August 1944
Burial Date: 21 August 1944
Race: W
Gender: M
Cemetery: Monongalia County, W.V. Cemetery

Name: Jack Harbar
Birth Date: 25 July 1893
Birth Place: Austria
Death Date: 15 April 1944
Burial Date: 17 April 1944
Race: W
Gender: M
Cemetery: Monongalia County, W.V. Cemetery

Name: Joe Horvat
Birth Date: Unknown
Birth Place: Hungary
Death Date: 29 March 1944
Burial Date: 01 April 1944
Race: W
Gender: M
Cemetery: Monongalia County, W.V. Cemetery


Name: Paul Kish
Birth Date: 25 January 1870
Birth Place: Unknown
Death Date: 24 January 1944
Burial Date: 25 January 1944
Race: W
Gender: M
Cemetery: Monongalia County, W.V. Cemetery


Name: Mike Kuloc
Birth Date: 1855
Birth Place: Russia
Death Date: 27 January 1944
Burial Date: 28 January 1944
Race: W
Gender: M
Cemetery: Monongalia County, W.V. Cemetery

Name: Frank Michnyiti
Birth Date: 27 April 1944
Birth Place: Fairmont State Hospital
Death Date: 01 August 1944
Burial Date: 02 August 1944
Race: W
Gender: M
Cemetery: Monongalia County, W.V. Cemetery


Name: Jacob Moskalevich
Birth Date: 1862
Birth Place: Russia
Death Date: 01 April 1944
Burial Date: 03 April 1944
Race: W
Gender: M
Cemetery: Monongalia County, W.V. Cemetery


Name: Mike Purse
Birth Date: 08 November 1873
Birth Place: Russia
Death Date: 09 June 1944
Burial Date: ----
Race: W
Gender: M
Cemetery: Monongalia County, W.V. Cemetery

Name: Mrs. Ora Thomas Ross
Birth Date: 1889
Birth Place: Virginia
Death Date: 03 July 1944
Burial Date: 06 July 1944
Race: N
Gender: F
Cemetery: Monongalia County, W.V. Cemetery


Name: Samuel Shaffer
Birth Date: Unknown
Birth Place: Unknown
Death Date: 05 April 1944
Burial Date: 07 April 1944
Race: W
Gender: M
Cemetery: Monongalia County, W.V. Cemetery


Name: Connie Mae Starkey
Birth Date: 01 December 1942
Birth Place: Sabraton, W.Va.
Death Date: 13 July 1944
Burial Date: 15 July 1944
Race: W
Gender: F
Cemetery: Monongalia County, W.V. Cemetery

Name: John Summers
Birth Date: 07 April 1853
Birth Place: Maryland
Death Date: 06 July 1944
Burial Date: 10 July 1944
Race: N
Gender:M
Cemetery: Monongalia County, W.V. Cemetery


Name: Alex Vardiy
Birth Date: Unknown
Birth Place: Austria- Hungary
Death Date: 23 April 1944
Burial Date: 26 April 1944
Race: W
Gender: M
Cemetery: Monongalia County, W.V. Cemetery


Name: Mike Verbin
Birth Date: 17 May 1895
Birth Place: Russia
Death Date: 17 January 1944
Burial Date: 20 January 1944
Race: W
Gender: M
Cemetery: Monongalia County, W.V. Cemetery

Name: William Young
Birth Date: Unknown
Birth Place: Unknown
Death Date: 14 September 1944
Burial Date: 20 September 1944
Race: B
Gender: M
Cemetery: Monongalia County, W.V. Cemetery

# 1945

Name: Peter Dargus
Birth Date: Unknown
Death Date: 25 December 1945
Burial Date: 27 December 1945
Race: W
Gender: M
Cemetery: Monongalia County, W.V. Cemetery


Name: John Hewitt
Birth Date: 04 May 1875
Birth Place: Frostburg, Maryland
Death Date: 08 November 1945
Burial Date: 10 November 1945
Race: W
Gender: M
Cemetery: Monongalia County, W.V. Cemetery


Name: Thomas Hewitt
Birth Date: 04 May 1875
Birth Place: Frostburg, Maryland
Death Date: 20 August 1945
Burial Date: 22 August 1945
Race: W
Gender: M
Cemetery: Monongalia County, W.V. Cemetery

Name: Mike Houseman
Birth Date: 29 September 1870
Birth Place: Poland
Death Date: 18 November 1945
Burial Date: 20 November 1945
Race: W
Gender: M
Cemetery: Monongalia County, W.V. Cemetery


Name: Alex Kendzel
Birth Date: 20 July 1872
Birth Place: Austria Hungary
Death Date: 19 June 1945
Burial Date: 20 June 1945
Race: W
Gender: M
Cemetery: Monongalia County, W.V. Cemetery


Name: Gabriel Kidor
Birth Date: Unknown
Birth Place: Unknown
Death Date: 16 September 1945
Burial Date: 21 September 1945
Race: W
Gender: M
Cemetery: Monongalia County, W.V. Cemetery

Name: Hans Larson
Birth Date: 06 July 1865
Birth Place: Istad, Sweden
Death Date:21 January 1945
Burial Date: 23 January 1945
Race: W
Gender: M
Cemetery: Monongalia County, W.V. Cemetery


Name: Frank Miller
Birth Date: March 1865
Birth Place: Pa.
Death Date: 15 May 1945
Burial Date: 16 May 1945
Race: W
Gender: M
Cemetery: Monongalia County, W.V. Cemetery


Name: Joe Ponder
Birth Date: Unknown
Birth Place: Unknown
Death Date: 27 May 1945
Burial Date: 30 May 1945
Race: W
Gender: M
Cemetery: Monongalia County, W.V. Cemetery

Name: Louis Vincent
Birth Date: April 1869
Birth Place: Hungary
Death Date: 07 January 1945
Burial Date: 08 January 1945
Race: W
Gender: M
Cemetery: Monongalia County, W.V. Cemetery


Name: Albert Wheatley
Birth Date: 16 February 1862
Birth Place: England
Death Date: 16 September 1945
Burial Date: 18 September 1945
Race: W
Gender: M
Cemetery: Monongalia County, W.V. Cemetery


Name: James Williams
Birth Date: 03 October 1891
Birth Place: Alabama
Death Date: 02 April 1945
Burial Date: 04 April 1945
Race: Negro
Gender: M
Cemetery: Monongalia County, W.V. Cemetery

Name: James Woods
Birth Date: 15 November 1869
Birth Place: Charlottesville, Virginia
Death Date: 16 February 1945
Burial Date: 17 February 1945
Race: C
Gender: M
Cemetery: Monongalia County, W.V. Cemetery

# 1946

Name: John Bednar
Birth Date: 17 May 1863
Birth Place: Hungary
Death Date: 11 January 1946
Burial Date: 14 January 1946
Race: W
Gender: M
Cemetery: Monongalia County, W.V. Cemetery


Name: Tony Endihar
Birth Date: 17 January 1879
Birth Place: Austria
Death Date: 22 April 1946
Burial Date: 25 April 1946
Race: W
Gender: M
Cemetery: Monongalia County, W.V. Cemetery


Name: Walter Fetsome
Birth Date: Unknown
Birth Place: Poland
Death Date: 07 September 1946
Burial Date: 11 September 1946
Race: W
Gender: M
Cemetery: Monongalia County, W.V. Cemetery

Name: Robert Filipevich
Birth Date: 1883
Birth Place: Yugoslavia
Death Date: 09 September 1946
Burial Date: 11 September 1946
Race: W
Gender: M
Cemetery: Monongalia County, W.V. Cemetery


Name: Thomas Fudder (Pudder?)
Birth Date: Unknown
Birth Place: Unknown
Death Date: 26 June 1946
Burial Date: 28 June 1946
Race: W
Gender: M
Cemetery: Monongalia County, W.V. Cemetery


Name: George Kolarik
Birth Date: 26 March 1870
Birth Place: Czechoslovakia
Death Date: 11 November 1946
Burial Date: 13 November 1946
Race: W
Gender: M
Cemetery: Monongalia County, W.V. Cemetery

Name: Frank Lopinski
Birth Date: May 1876
Birth Place: Poland
Death Date: 09 November 1946
Burial Date: 12 November 1946
Race: W
Gender: M
Cemetery: Monongalia County, W.V. Cemetery


Name: John Merslovich
Birth Date: 20 October 1879
Birth Place: Yugoslavia
Death Date: 19 June 1946
Burial Date: 22 June 1946
Race: W
Gender: M
Cemetery: Monongalia County, W.V. Cemetery


Name: Dan Sheveloff
Birth Date: 1880
Birth Place: Russia
Death Date: 09 September 1946
Burial Date: 11 September 1946
Race: W
Gender: M
Cemetery: Monongalia County, W.V. Cemetery

Name: Albert Sych
Birth Date: 01 March 1875
Birth Place: Hungary
Death Date: 01 April 1946
Burial Date: 03 April 1946
Race: W
Gender: M
Cemetery: Monongalia County, W.V. Cemetery


Name: John Vizing
Birth Date: 20 June 1869
Birth Place: Lithuania
Death Date: 08 September 1946
Burial Date: 10 September 1946
Race: W
Gender: M
Cemetery: Monongalia County, W.V. Cemetery


Name: Peter Zhoza
Birth Date: Unknown
Birth Place: Unknown
Death Date: 02 March 1946
Burial Date: 06 March 1946
Race: W
Gender: M
Cemetery: Monongalia County, W.V. Cemetery

# 1947

## 1947

Name: Paul Billy
Birth Date: 10 January 1879
Birth Place: Austria
Death Date: 19 December 1947
Burial Date: December 1947
Race: W
Gender: M
Cemetery: Monongalia County, W.V. Cemetery


Name: James Byrd
Birth Date: Unknown
Birth Place: Virginia
Death Date: 21 April 1947
Burial Date: 23 April 1947
Race: Negro
Gender: M
Cemetery: Monongalia County, W.V. Cemetery

Name: Charles Cheasko
Birth Date: 04 February 1857
Birth Place: Lithuania
Death Date: 13 August 1947
Burial Date: 14 August 1947
Race: W
Gender: M
Cemetery: Monongalia County, W.V. Cemetery

Name: Laslo Denes (Louis Dinch)
Birth Date: 30 August 1875
Birth Place: Hungary
Death Date: 18 November 1947
Burial Date: 21 November 1947
Race: W
Gender: M
Cemetery: Monongalia County, W.V. Cemetery


Name: John Dufoski
Birth Date: 01 June 1868
Birth Place: Russia
Death Date: 14 May 1947
Burial Date: 14 May 1947
Race: W
Gender: M
Cemetery: Monongalia County, W.V. Cemetery


Name: Andy Feyerchak
Birth Date: 15 May 1872
Birth Place: Czechoslovakia
Death Date: 31 May 1947
Burial Date: 02 June 1947
Race: W
Gender: M
Cemetery: Monongalia County, W.V. Cemetery

Name: Pedro Fortea
Birth Date: 01 October 1890
Birth Place: Spain
Death Date: 14 April 1947
Burial Date: 16 April 1947
Race: W
Gender: M
Cemetery: Monongalia County, W.V. Cemetery


Name: Isaac Harden
Birth Date: 20 June 1866
Birth Place: Hopwood, Pa.
Death Date: 31 December 1947
Burial Date: 01 January 1948
Race: W
Gender: M
Cemetery: Monongalia County, W.V. Cemetery


Name: Jack Hurd
Birth Date: 18 March 1877
Birth Place: Alabama
Death Date: 07 November 1947
Burial Date: 09 November 1947
Race: C
Gender: M
Cemetery: Monongalia County, W.V. Cemetery

Name: Charles Edward Hyatt
Birth Date: 28 October 1947
Birth Place: Mona, W.Va.
Death Date: 31 October 1947
Burial Date: 01 November 1947
Race: W
Gender: M
Cemetery: Monongalia County, W.V. Cemetery


Name: Jack Masuck
Birth Date: Unknown
Birth Place: Russia
Death Date: 08 July 1947
Burial Date: 11 July 1947
Race: W
Gender: M
Cemetery: Monongalia County, W.V. Cemetery


Name: Nick Nicholas
Birth Date: Unknown
Birth Place: Russia
Death Date: 01 June 1947
Burial Date: 03 June 1947
Race: W
Gender: M
Cemetery: Monongalia County, W.V. Cemetery

Name: George Priglopan
Birth Date: 1873
Birth Place: Austria
Death Date: 22 February 1947
Burial Date: 26 February 1947
Race: W
Gender: M
Cemetery: Monongalia County, W.V. Cemetery


Name: Samuel Asbury Wright
Birth Date: 07 March 1865
Birth Place: Monongalia County, W.Va.
Death Date: 11 July 1947
Burial Date: 14 July 1947
Race: W
Gender: M
Cemetery: Monongalia County, W.V. Cemetery

# 1948

Name: Paul Bara
Birth Date: Unknown
Birth Place: Dalmatia
Death Date: 17 March 1948
Burial Date: 23 March 1948
Race: W
Gender: M
Cemetery: Monongalia County, W.V. Cemetery


Name: John Bartasevich (Barrtosicia)
Birth Date: Unknown
Birth Place: Lithuania
Death Date: 04 April 1948
Burial Date: 06 April 1948
Race: W
Gender: M
Cemetery: Monongalia County, W.V. Cemetery

Name: Frank Boycus
Birth Date: 1866
Birth Place: Hungary
Death Date: 09 March 1948
Burial Date: 13 March 1948
Race: W
Gender: M
Cemetery: Monongalia County, W.V. Cemetery

Name: John Brevich
Birth Date: 10 June 1878
Birth Place: Yugoslavia
Death Date: 04 January 1948
Burial Date: 06 January 1948
Race: W
Gender: M
Cemetery: Monongalia County, W.V. Cemetery


Name: William Golla
Birth Date: 14 May 1872
Birth Place: Poland
Death Date: 18 October 1948
Burial Date: 20 October 1948
Race: W
Gender: M
Cemetery: Monongalia County, W.V. Cemetery

Name: Jacob Holerski
Birth Date: 02 November 1878
Birth Place: Poland
Death Date: 11 January 1948
Burial Date: 13 January 1948
Race: W
Gender: M
Cemetery: Monongalia County, W.V. Cemetery


Name: Andrew Horosky
Birth Date: Unknown
Birth Place: Hungary
Death Date: 15 June 1948
Burial Date: 16 June 1948
Race: W
Gender: M
Cemetery: Monongalia County, W.V. Cemetery


Name: Louis Labish
Birth Date: 23 September 1876
Birth Place: Hungary
Death Date: 26 March 1948
Burial Date: 27 March 1948
Race: W
Gender: M
Cemetery: Monongalia County, W.V. Cemetery

Name: William Lemasters
Birth Date: 05 July 1878
Birth Place: Unknown
Death Date: 25 October 1948
Burial Date: 08 November 1948
Race: W
Gender: M
Cemetery: Monongalia County, W.V. Cemetery

Name: Rose Merrill
Birth Date: 14 December 1872
Birth Place: Jacksonburg, W.Va.
Death Date: 30 January 1948
Burial Date: 02 February 1948
Race: W
Gender: F
Cemetery: Monongalia County, W.V. Cemetery


Name: Michael Smuler
Birth Date: Unknown
Birth Place: Unknown
Death Date: 08 April 1948
Burial Date: 14 April 1948
Race: W
Gender: M
Cemetery: Monongalia County, W.V. Cemetery

Name: Tony Spadafore
Birth Date: Unknown
Birth Place: Italy
Death Date: 11 February 1948
Burial Date: 14 February 1948
Race: W
Gender: M
Cemetery: Monongalia County, W.V. Cemetery

Name: August Szency
Birth Date: 18 December 1873
Birth Place: Hungary
Death Date: 21 June 1948
Burial Date: 23 June 1948
Race: W
Gender: M
Cemetery: Monongalia County, W.V. Cemetery


Name: Rose Ann Williams
Birth Date: 10 February 1948
Birth Place: Monongalia County, W.Va.
Death Date: 17 February 1948
Burial Date: 20 February 1948
Race: W
Gender: F
Cemetery: Monongalia County, W.V. Cemetery

# 1949

Name: Lance Bohut
Birth Date: 04 April 1882
Birth Place: Czechoslovakia
Death Date: 24 December 1949
Burial Date: 27 December 1949
Race: W
Gender: M
Cemetery: Monongalia County, W.V. Cemetery


Name: Charles Burkas
Birth Date: 1877
Birth Place: Hungary
Death Date: 09 August 1949
Burial Date: 12 August 1949
Race: W
Gender: M
Cemetery: Monongalia County, W.V. Cemetery

Name: Frank Carpenter
Birth Date: 30 July 1866
Birth Place: W.Va.
Death Date: 13 October 1949
Burial Date: 15 October 1949
Race: W
Gender: M
Cemetery: Monongalia County, W.V. Cemetery

Name: William J. Carpenter
Birth Date: 02 October 1882
Birth Place: Orange County, Va.
Death Date: 11 February 1949
Burial Date: 12 February 1949
Race: W
Gender: M
Cemetery: Monongalia County, W.V. Cemetery


Name: Joe Gallo
Birth Date: Unknown
Birth Place: Italy
Death Date: 01 December 1949
Burial Date: ----
Race: W
Gender: M
Cemetery: Monongalia County, W.V. Cemetery

Name: Joe Hamrick
Birth Date: 28 December 1906
Birth Place: W.Va.
Death Date: 01 August 1949
Burial Date: 04 August 1949
Race: W
Gender: M
Cemetery: Monongalia County, W.V. Cemetery


Name: Betty Hurd
Birth Date: 30 March 1890
Birth Place: Pa.
Death Date: 12 April 1949
Burial Date: 17 April 1949
Race: C
Gender: F
Cemetery: Monongalia County, W.V. Cemetery


Name: Jake Kozakiewiez
Birth Date: 15 May 1870
Birth Place: Russia
Death Date: 25 February 1949
Burial Date: 29 February 1949
Race: W
Gender: M
Cemetery: Monongalia County, W.V. Cemetery

Name: Frank Luko
Birth Date: 01 October 1861
Birth Place: Austria Hungary
Death Date: 16 February 1949
Burial Date: 19 February 1949
Race: W
Gender: M
Cemetery: Monongalia County, W.V. Cemetery


Name: Louis Nevels
Birth Date: 1883
Birth Place: Unknown
Death Date: 17 April 1949
Burial Date: 20 April 1949
Race: C
Gender: M
Cemetery: Monongalia County, W.V. Cemetery


Name: Teleshore Romanville
Birth Date: 21 November 1875
Birth Place: Belgium
Death Date: 14 June 1949
Burial Date: 16 June 1949
Race: W
Gender: M
Cemetery: Monongalia County, W.V. Cemetery

Name: John Tolarick
Birth Date: 10 April 1878
Birth Place: Poland
Death Date: 23 December 1949
Burial Date: 24 December 1949
Race: W
Gender: M
Cemetery: Monongalia County, W.V. Cemetery


Name: Genevieve Watson
Birth Date: 10 June 1885
Birth Place: Montgomery, W.Va.
Death Date: 12 November 1949
Burial Date: 15 November 1949
Race: W
Gender: F
Cemetery: Monongalia County, W.V. Cemetery

# 1950

Name: Mike Antoniak
Birth Date: Unknown
Birth Place: "Foreign"
Death Date: 27 May 1950
Burial Date: 31 May 1950
Race: W
Gender: M
Cemetery: Monongalia County, W.V. Cemetery


Name: Jacob Gummerson
Birth Date: 09 March 1908
Birth Place: Dunbar, Fayette County, Pa.
Death Date: 31 January 1950
Burial Date: 03 February 1950
Race: W
Gender: M
Cemetery: Monongalia County, W.V. Cemetery

Name: Sam Jacobs
Birth Date: 02 February 1875
Birth Place: Russia
Death Date: 15 August 1950
Burial Date: 17 August 1950
Race: W
Gender: M
Cemetery: Monongalia County, W.V. Cemetery


Name: Chanie Lindsay
Birth Date: 08 December 1898
Birth Place: Virginia
Death Date: 16 July 1950
Burial Date: 18 July 1950
Race: W
Gender: M
Cemetery: Monongalia County, W.V. Cemetery


Name: John Loharne
Birth Date: Unknown
Birth Place: Yugoslavia
Death Date: 21 February 1950
Burial Date: 25 February 1950
Race: W
Gender: M
Cemetery: Monongalia County, W.V. Cemetery

Name: Carl Maranoff
Birth Date: 1870
Birth Place: Russia
Death Date: 03 September 1950
Burial Date: 06 September 1950
Race: W
Gender: M
Cemetery: Monongalia County, W.V. Cemetery


Name: Patsy Matsy
Birth Date: 1880
Birth Place: Italy
Death Date: 02 January 1950
Burial Date: 06 January 1950
Race: W
Gender: M
Cemetery: Monongalia County, W.V. Cemetery


Name: Margaret Lease Miller
Birth Date: 15 December 1924
Birth Place: Lonaconing, Maryland
Death Date: 08 July 1950
Burial Date: 11 July 1950
Race: W
Gender: F
Cemetery: Monongalia County, W.V. Cemetery

Name: Steve Shuka
Birth Date: 24 December 1885
Birth Place: Austria
Death Date: 23 June 1950
Burial Date: 26 June 1950
Race: W
Gender: M
Cemetery: Monongalia County, W.V. Cemetery

Name: Mary Strosnider
Birth Date: 16 July 1880
Birth Place: Greene County, Pennsylvania
Death Date: 17 April 1950
Burial Date: 19 April 1950
Race: W
Gender: M
Cemetery: Monongalia County, W.V. Cemetery

Name: Joe Toth
Birth Date: 28 November 1863
Birth Place: Hungary
Death Date: 27 May 1950
Burial Date: 31 May 1950
Race: W
Gender: M
Cemetery: Monongalia County, W.V. Cemetery

Name: Dollar Bill Williams
Birth Date: 06 May 1834
Birth Place: Africa
Death Date: 18 December 1950
Burial Date: 21 December 1950
Race: African
Gender: M
Cemetery: Monongalia County, W.V. Cemetery

# 1951

Name: John Nicklosh
Birth Date: Unknown
Birth Place: Russia
Death Date: 19 July 1951
Burial Date: 23 July 1951
Race: W
Gender: M
Cemetery: Monongalia County, W.V. Cemetery


Name: Stanley Pawlecki
Birth Date: 1869
Birth Place: Poland
Death Date: 17 December 1951
Burial Date: 20 December 1951
Race: W
Gender: M
Cemetery: Monongalia County, W.V. Cemetery


Name: Tony Zagmont
Birth Date: 12 July 1881
Birth Place: Poland
Death Date: 29 March 1951
Burial Date: 31 March 1951
Race: W
Gender: M
Cemetery: Monongalia County, W.V. Cemetery

Name: Frank Kreskai
Birth Date: 1870
Birth Place: Hungary
Death Date: 14 February 1951
Burial Date: 16 February 1951
Race: W
Gender: M
Cemetery: Monongalia County, W.V. Cemetery


Name: George C. Merrill
Birth Date: 10 June 1903
Birth Place: Wetzel County, W.Va.
Death Date: 31 May 1951
Burial Date: 02 June 1951
Race: W
Gender: M
Cemetery: Monongalia County, W.V. Cemetery


Name: Mike Vebek
Birth Date: 15 September 1882
Birth Place: Czechoslovakia
Death Date: 08 May 1951
Burial Date: 10 May 1951
Race: W
Gender: M
Cemetery: Monongalia County, W.V. Cemetery

Name: Charles Kosick
Birth Date: Unknown
Birth Place: Russia
Death Date: 17May 1951
Race: W
Gender: M
Cemetery: Monongalia County, W.V. Cemetery


Name: Richard Collins
Birth Date: 1889
Birth Place: Ala.
Death Date: 14 June 1951
Burial Date: 19 June 1951
Race: Negro
Gender: M
Cemetery: Monongalia County, W.V. Cemetery

# 1952

Name: Vassel Charles Dubeno
Birth Date: 1880
Birth Place: Russia
Death Date:17 July 1952
Burial Date: 21 July 1952
Race: W
Gender: M
Cemetery: Monongalia County, W.V. Cemetery


Name: Granville Moneypenny
Birth Date: 25 December 1863
Birth Place: Unknown
Death Date: 21 March 1952
Burial Date: 23 March 1952
Race: W
Gender: M
Cemetery: Monongalia County, W.V. Cemetery


Name: Stephen Mikisanovich
Birth Date: 07 July 1873
Birth Place: Yugoslavia
Death Date: 18 September 1952
Burial Date: 22 September 1952
Race: W
Gender: M
Cemetery: Monongalia County, W.V. Cemetery

Name: Mike Koshki
Birth Date: 29 October 1880
Birth Place: Russia
Death Date: 06 December 1952
Burial Date: 09 December 1952
Race: W
Gender: M
Cemetery: Monongalia County, W.V. Cemetery


Name: John Sance
Birth Date: Unknown
Birth Place: Hungary
Death Date: 26 May 1952
Burial Date: 29 May 1952
Race: W
Gender: M
Cemetery: Monongalia County, W.V. Cemetery

# 1953

Name: Florian Citula
Birth Date: 1881
Birth Place: Romania
Death Date: 03 May 1953
Burial Date: 06 May 1953
Race: W
Gender: M
Cemetery: Monongalia County, W.V. Cemetery


Name: John Smith Dopierela
Birth Date: 19 October 1885
Birth Place: Poland
Death Date: 15 March 1953
Burial Date: 17 March 1953
Race: W
Gender: M
Cemetery: Monongalia County, W.V. Cemetery

Name: Mary Lada
Birth Date: 01 January 1883
Birth Place: Poland
Death Date: 19 February 1953
Burial Date: 23 February 1953
Race: W
Gender: F
Cemetery: Monongalia County, W.V. Cemetery


Name: Frank Landis
Birth Date: 25 March 1874
Birth Place: Hungary
Death Date: 24 February 1953
Burial Date: 27 February 1953
Race: W
Gender: M
Cemetery: Monongalia County, W.V. Cemetery


Name: Martin Mikulsky
Birth Date: Unknown
Birth Place: Unknown
Death Date: 10 June 1953
Burial Date: 13 June 1953
Race: W
Gender: M
Cemetery: Monongalia County, W.V. Cemetery

Name: Media Sophia Provance
Birth Date: 27 August 1874
Birth Place: Greensboro, Pa.
Death Date: 04 April 1953
Burial Date: 11 April 1953
Race: W
Gender: F
Cemetery: Monongalia County, W.V. Cemetery


Name: Serrano Rojo
Birth Date: 27 May 1879
Birth Place: Spain
Death Date: 20 August 1953
Burial Date: 24 August 1953
Race: W
Gender: M
Cemetery: Monongalia County, W.V. Cemetery


Name: Melvina Sample
Birth Date: October 1874
Birth Place: Atlanta, Georgia
Death Date: 01 April 1953
Burial Date: 04 April 1953
Race: Negro
Gender: F
Cemetery: Monongalia County, W.V. Cemetery

# 1954

Name: Frank Shine
Birth Date: 09 August 1873
Birth Place: Austria
Death Date: 28 November 1954
Burial Date: 30 November 1954
Race: W
Gender: M
Cemetery: Monongalia County, W.V. Cemetery


Name: John Sobo
Birth Date: 1880
Birth Place: Hungary
Death Date: 28 August 1954
Burial Date: 30 August 1954
Race: W
Gender: M
Cemetery: Monongalia County, W.V. Cemetery

Name: Cleveland Stokes
Birth Date: 10 March 1885
Birth Place: Virginia
Death Date: 18 September 1954
Burial Date: 22 September 1954
Race: W
Gender: M
Cemetery: Monongalia County, W.V. Cemetery


Name: Susie Bogart
Birth Date: 13 June 1905
Birth Place: Lincoln County, W.Va.
Death Date: 28 November 1954
Burial Date: 30 November 1954
Race: W
Gender: F
Cemetery: Monongalia County, W.V. Cemetery


Name: John Uhlman
Birth Date: 24 December 1879
Birth Place: Hungary
Death Date: 28 April 1954
Burial Date: 30 April 1954
Race: W
Gender: M
Cemetery: Monongalia County, W.V. Cemetery

Name: John Pappas
Birth Date: 1874
Birth Place: Greece
Death Date: 25 March 1954
Burial Date: 29 March 1954
Race: W
Gender: M
Cemetery: Monongalia County, W.V. Cemetery

# 1955

Name: Lindsay Boxley
Birth Date: 08 September 1882
Birth Place: Virginia
Death Date: 28 July 1955
Burial Date: 29 July 1955
Race: Colored
Gender: M
Cemetery: Monongalia County, W.V. Cemetery


Name: Walter Crankasky
Birth Date: 1885
Birth Place: Poland
Death Date: 14 January 1955
Burial Date: 17 January 1955
Race: W
Gender: M
Cemetery: Monongalia County, W.V. Cemetery

Name: Santo Sam Gillvotti
Birth Date: October 1880
Birth Place: Italy
Death Date: 15 November 1955
Burial Date: 19 November 1955
Race: W
Gender: M
Cemetery: Monongalia County, W.V. Cemetery


Name: Jack Kotar
Birth Date: 1893
Birth Place: Unknown
Death Date: 25 July 1955
Burial Date: 25 July 1955
Race: W
Gender: M
Cemetery: Monongalia County, W.V. Cemetery


Name: John Lutran
Birth Date: 15 January 1880
Birth Place: Hungary
Death Date: 23 February 1955
Burial Date: 25 February 1955
Race: W
Gender: M
Cemetery: Monongalia County, W.V. Cemetery

Name: Ignatz Norris
Birth Date: 30 June 1879
Birth Place: Lithuania
Death Date: 03 August 1955
Burial Date: 06 August 1955
Race: W
Gender: M
Cemetery: Monongalia County, W.V. Cemetery


Name: Matt Patrovich
Birth Date: 21 September 1882
Birth Place: Yugoslavia
Death Date: 06 October 1955
Burial Date: 18 October 1955
Race: W
Gender: M
Cemetery: Monongalia County, W.V. Cemetery


Name: Mike Rubish
Birth Date: 1883
Birth Place: Unknown
Death Date: 27 December 1955
Burial Date:  30 December 1955
Race: W
Gender: M
Cemetery: Monongalia County, W.V. Cemetery

Name: Joseph Sherospsky
Birth Date: March 1874
Birth Place: Poland
Death Date: 17 July 1955
Burial Date: 19 July 1955
Race: W
Gender: M
Cemetery: Monongalia County, W.V. Cemetery


Name: Raymond Sowchok
Birth Date: 14 October 1879
Birth Place: Russia
Death Date: 17 March 1955
Burial Date: 19 March 1955
Race: W
Gender: M
Cemetery: Monongalia County, W.V. Cemetery

## ABOUT THE AUTHOR

Cynthia (Cindie) Harper was born in Morgantown, West Virginia. She earned a Bachelor and Master of Social Work Degree from West Virginia University. She is the Director of Historical Research at Sweet Springs Resort Park Foundation. Harper lived in Hawaii for many years but eventually allowed those country roads to take her back home to West Virginia.

www.ingramcontent.com/pod-product-compliance
Lightning Source LLC
Chambersburg PA
CBHW052129270326
41930CB00012B/2819